Guide to

Greenhouse Gardening

Guide to
Greenhouse
Gardening

Alan Titchmarsh

BOOKS

For Alison

The publishers would like to thank the following for supplying colour photographs:
Pat Brindley, The Harry Smith Horticultural Photographic Collection and Brian Furner.

Thanks are also due to *Alton Greenhouses* for supplying the greenhouse used on
the cover, endpapers and title page.

Photographs on cover, endpapers and title page by *Paul Williams.*

Illustrations by *Tony Streek*, except for those on pages 14 and 15, *Chris Forsey*,
pages 64, 74, 78, 84 and 90, *Joyce Tuhill* and page 96 *Angela Lewer.*

Published for The Boots Company Limited by
The Hamlyn Publishing Group Limited
London · New York · Sydney · Toronto
Astronaut House, Feltham, Middlesex, England
© Copyright The Hamlyn Publishing Group Limited 1980
ISBN 0 600 34131 3

Phototypeset in England by Tradespools Limited, Frome, Somerset
in 10 on 11pt Garamond

Printed and bound in Spain by Graficromo, S.A. - Córdoba

Contents

What makes a good greenhouse?

Choosing a greenhouse is like choosing a car; all models fulfil the same purpose but they vary in size, shape, performance and cost. Scan the advertisement pages of a gardening magazine or inspect the display of greenhouses at a local garden centre and you may be left in a state of confusion because there are so many types available. Don't worry – answer the following questions and you should be able to narrow the choice to just one or two greenhouses tailor-made to your requirements.

What will it look like?

Make sure you buy a greenhouse you can live with. However technically advanced a certain design may be you will soon become irritated if it offends your eye. Most greenhouses will last for several decades so choose one that will look good in your garden when the trees and plants are mature.

How much does it cost?

Only you know what you can afford. Greenhouses made by reputable manufacturers are well-constructed and durable and should give you good return for your money. It is seldom worth making your own greenhouse nowadays because timber and glass are so expensive. If you are short of money consider buying a polythene greenhouse which will last until you can afford a more permanent structure.

How big should it be?

Having chosen a greenhouse that fits your pocket, make sure that it will also fit your garden and the plants you want to grow. However large your greenhouse may seem at the outset it will not be long before it is full, so choose the largest model your garden can accommodate.

What will it be used for?

Once you have sorted out what you require of your greenhouse it's time to consider the needs of the plants. If tomatoes, chrysanthemums and other tall growers are to be housed a glass-to-ground model will admit more light. Pot plants are more easily grown on some kind of staging which presents them at waist height. In these circumstances it is not necessary to have glass right down to ground level. Half-timbered sides will provide better insulation against winter cold and will hide from view watering cans, pots and other equipment stored beneath the staging. Most gardeners want to grow pot plants *and* tomatoes, so a greenhouse which is glazed to ground level on one side and half-timbered on the other is a good solution; so too is a model with a very low wooden 'wall' on all sides.

Will it let in enough light and air?

If you grow a plant in a greenhouse that admits little light it will become tall, pale, spindly and too weak to resist pest and disease attack. If you grow it in a greenhouse with a stagnant atmosphere two main problems arise: fungus diseases will thrive in the still, damp air, and bright sunshine will raise the temperature to such an extent that the leaves of plants will become scorched and brown. A good greenhouse should avoid both these problems. A thin but strong wooden or aluminium framework means that the panes of glass can be a good size and so admit plenty of light, and ventilators both in the ridge and the sides of the house will keep the air circulating – so maintaining a healthy atmosphere while allowing unwanted heat to escape in summer.

Many polythene greenhouses can only be ventilated by opening the doors at each end to create a through-draught; the longer the greenhouse the less effective is this type of ventilation.

Make sure that air can get into the greenhouse only when you want it to. Icy draughts in winter can be as damaging as a lack of air in summer, so doors and ventilators should fit snugly.

Is it strong?

Look for a greenhouse with a well-made framework that is securely fastened together. Try to examine one that has been erected so that you can see just how tough it is. Having satisfied yourself that the greenhouse itself is strong, do make sure that it is firmly attached to sound foundations which give it an even footing. However heavy your greenhouse may seem to you a strong wind can make light work of blowing it over the rooftops. Polythene greenhouses rely entirely on firm anchorage for strength and stability.

Can you get into it?

The narrower the greenhouse, the narrower the door. This raises problems not just for gardeners who are generously built but also for those who want to barrow in compost, soil, gravel etc. Greenhouses are available with double doors to make wheelbarrow access easy, and with extra-tall doors to allow more headroom.

An impressive display created by clever choice of flowers and foliage

Choice of material

Over the years manufacturers have tried out numerous materials for greenhouse construction from reinforced concrete to heavy steel. Thankfully the choice nowadays is mainly confined to timber and aluminium alloy. Both these materials look smart and are strong enough to give years of service, but they must be treated differently.

Wood

The best timber greenhouses are made of western red cedar, a rot-resistant and very durable wood from North America. Cedar does not need painting but should be treated with a water repellant such as Red Cedar Preservative or linseed oil to prolong its life. Many greenhouses are dipped in the preservative before being sold; others are supplied with a tinful of the product which you will have to brush on before putting the sections together. If preservative is applied every couple of years your greenhouse will last a lifetime.

Some manufacturers are now producing softwood greenhouses as a cheaper alternative to their cedarwood range. A number of timbers are used and due to their less resilient nature they must first be treated with primer and then coated with exterior-quality paint.

Not all timber greenhouses rely on putty to keep their glass in place. Many are now equipped with grooves into which the glass is slotted, so making the replacement of broken panes much simpler. It is easy to fix things up inside a wooden greenhouse; a well-placed nail will support a thermometer or training wire. Attaching these to the inside of an aluminium house can present problems.

Finally, wood seems to have one big advantage – it looks mellow and natural and can fit into any garden with the greatest of ease.

Aluminium

Aluminium is the material a busy gardener should choose. Apart from costing less than their wooden counterparts, aluminium greenhouses need no maintenance – other than the oiling of moving parts – and glazing is easily accomplished with the aid of snap-on sprigs or plastic strips.

That said, many manufacturers supply aluminium greenhouses in very basic kit form – you will first have to construct each section of the house and then bolt them all together. Check that comprehensive instructions are available before you buy.

Shortly after the house has been erected a white powdery deposit will appear. This minor corrosion is expected and causes no problems. In seaside localities, however, it may be more pronounced and you might be better advised to choose a timber greenhouse. Seek the advice of local gardeners before you decide, or alternatively buy an aluminium greenhouse which has been coated with white or green acrylic paint.

Glass or plastic?

If you are investing in a permanent structure then glass is the obvious choice. It lasts indefinitely unless accidentally broken; it retains heat more effectively than plastic so fuel bills will be smaller; it lets in the maximum amount of light; it can be coated with shading compounds and is easily cleaned.

Plastic is the material to choose for temporary structures and small mobile greenhouses that can be

A traditional wooden greenhouse may need to be painted with preservative before construction.

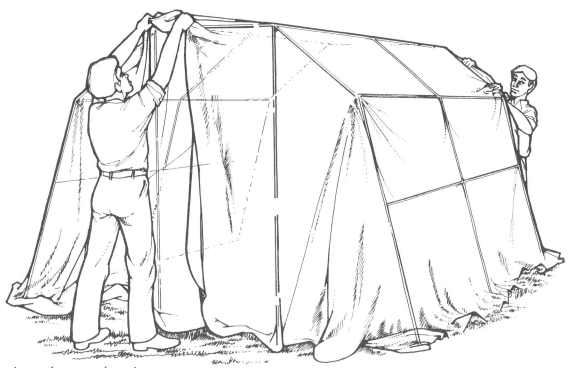

The plastic tunnel type greenhouse is quick and simple to construct. Here the plastic envelope is being drawn over the framework.

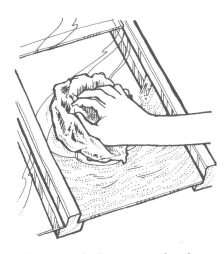

Electrostatic shading compound can be removed with a duster when dry.

moved around the garden and planted exactly where you want them at a particular time. Plastic greenhouses are normally made from 600 gauge polythene sheeting supported by a tubular aluminium alloy framework. The 'envelope', as it is called, is stretched over the frame and its edges buried in the ground to give the house stability.

Where children are at large plastic is a safe alternative to glass, though as far as the plants are concerned it admits less light, allows heat to escape more quickly (especially if the plastic is corrugated) and collects condensation. The last problem can be overcome by spraying the inside of the house with a product called Sun Clear which causes the water to run off rather than hang in droplets.

Ventilation can be difficult to achieve in polythene tunnels where the doors are the only means of admitting air, but only in very long structures are severe problems likely to be encountered.

The biggest disadvantage of plastic – whether rigid or flexible – is its short life. Polythene will have to be renewed at least every two years when it becomes discoloured and brittle. All types of plastic collect dirt. Some of the rigid plastics now on the market are guaranteed for ten years, but they must still be regarded as temporary.

Despite these drawbacks plastic still has its place in the garden, and one advantage that a polythene house will always have over one made of glass is its low cost.

Siting your greenhouse

Finding the right place for your greenhouse need not be difficult, even if your garden is a small one. Provided that certain guidelines are followed you can look forward to growing healthy plants and tasty crops with the minimum of trouble.

Planning permission

Many local authorities do not insist on planning permission being obtained for greenhouses, but do check with them first in case the structure has to be sited a certain distance from your boundary fence. Remember, too, that a lean-to greenhouse may well mean an increase in rates.

Good light

Avoid building a greenhouse on a north-facing slope, and never build one on ground heavily overshadowed by buildings or trees. As well as casting shade, trees will foul the glass and gutters with their leaves in autumn, and they may harbour pests and diseases which are equally partial to the plants grown in your greenhouse.

Greenfly in trees will secrete sticky honeydew and if this lands on greenhouse glass it will collect dirt and grime. Should a heavy branch be blown from an overhanging tree in windy weather your greenhouse may well be flattened.

Shelter

If the trees are some distance away from the greenhouse they can be used to advantage as windbreaks. On very exposed sites greenhouses may be damaged by wind, and fuel bills will be dramatically increased as the heating system tries to keep pace with falling temperatures.

Frost pockets

Dips and hollows in the land are sometimes known as frost pockets. This is because cold air always collects in them – like water it always finds the lowest level. Build your greenhouse at the foot of a slope and your plants will make a slower start in spring. Heating bills will be higher too. If possible, build on level ground; here the foundations will be easier and

cheaper to construct. If you have to build on a slope, choose a spot half way down – avoiding the exposed position at the top and the frost pocket at the bottom.

Drainage

Make sure that the land on which you build is well drained. This will enable you to cultivate the greenhouse border soil at any time of year without it being too sticky.

Laying on services

A greenhouse sited fairly near your dwelling house is that much easier and cheaper to equip with water, electricity and, if you choose it for heating, gas. Consider installing the first two if at all possible – they will save you a lot of time and energy.

Accessibility

The nearer the greenhouse is to your back door the more comfortable it will be to reach in cold or wet weather. A gravel or slab path laid from door to door will help keep your feet clean.

Orientation

It is often suggested that the traditional span roof greenhouse should be positioned in the garden so that its ridge runs from east to west. This advice may be worth following when a very long greenhouse is being erected or where plenty of space is available. In a small garden follow the other guidelines given on this page and you will obtain good results from your greenhouse whatever its orientation. Choose the wall for a lean-to greenhouse very carefully. Those with south- and west-facing aspects will grow the widest range of plants, but many shade lovers will thrive in a lean-to with a northerly or easterly aspect.

A bad site, overshadowed by trees and an inconvenient distance from the house

A well-sited greenhouse

Types of greenhouse

Span-roof, glazed to the ground

The span-roofed greenhouse has two roof sections which are of equal size and slope down to the same level. The fully glazed version is particularly useful for it lets in the maximum amount of light right down to the ground. This is the greenhouse to buy if you plan to grow tomatoes, chrysanthemums or winter lettuce in the soil borders. Alternatively, choose a model glazed to the ground on only one side if you also want to grow plants in pots.

If this greenhouse is to be built on a lawn, surround it with a narrow path to prevent the mower from doing any damage. Both wooden and aluminium glass-to-ground greenhouses are available.

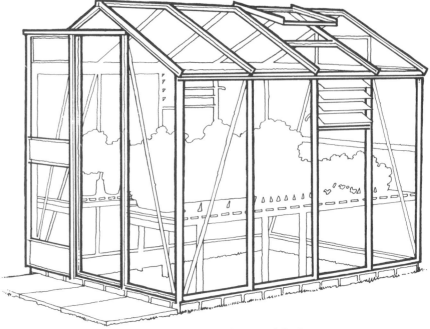

Span-roofed, glass-to-ground greenhouse

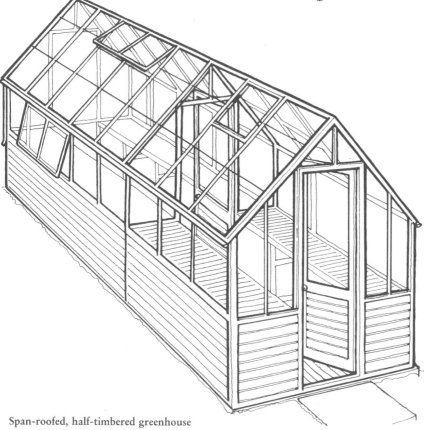

Span-roofed, half-timbered greenhouse

Span-roof, half-timbered

Of similar design to the glass-to-ground model, this greenhouse differs in that the sides are constructed of overlapping timber for the first 60 to 90 cm (2 to 3 ft) above ground level. If pot plants are to be your speciality this design has several advantages: the wooden sides retain heat better than glass, they hide from view the staging supports and also any watering cans, heating apparatus or plant pots which are stored on the floor.

There is a compromise between this greenhouse and the type glazed to ground level – models are available with very low wooden walls or with one side glazed to the ground and the other half-timbered.

The type shown here is made of timber, though aluminium versions with solid lower panels are also available.

Dutch type

The Dutch style greenhouse was developed, as its name suggests, in Holland and is much used in nurseries in Britain and Europe. The smaller versions offered to amateurs still possess the good features of their larger counterparts – sturdy construction, large panes of glass about 1.5 m by 75 cm (5 by 2½ ft) which allow good light transmission, and putty-less glazing. Set against this the panes are rather expensive to replace when broken, and the sloping sides of the greenhouse prevent tall plants from being positioned right against the glass. Cucumbers, melons and vines, however, can be trained on wires which slope parallel to the sides.

The true Dutch house is always made of timber, but aluminium greenhouses of almost identical design are now offered by one or two manufacturers.

Dutch light greenhouse

Multispan

These are a pleasing design, not too 'way out' to fit harmoniously into most gardens. The angle of the roof panels was developed to allow maximum light transmission, and the internal supports are very neat and take up no floor space.

Lean-to, half-timbered and glass-to-ground models are available so you should be able to pick one that suits your purpose, but in very small gardens you may find that the free-standing types are wider than you can cope with. However, if you have room for one you will discover that the staging is also generously wide. While this does mean that it may not be very easy to reach the back, it allows more plants to be fitted in.

All three designs are made in aluminium.

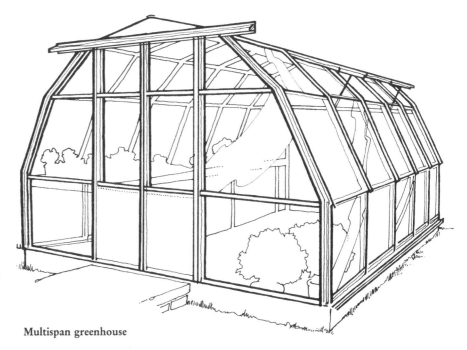

Multispan greenhouse

Types of greenhouse

Octagonal greenhouse

Octagonal

Just the job for modest plots, this greenhouse occupies a small area of ground but will contain a surprisingly large number of plants. Once you are inside, everything is at your elbow – a great boon to disabled gardeners who should choose a double-doored model to allow them easy access with a wheelchair. Check that the ventilators are a reasonable size. Most models make adequate provision for a change of air but on one or two only the small cone-like capping at the top can be lifted and this alone is not enough.

Octagonal houses are available in both aluminium and timber.

Dome-shaped greenhouse

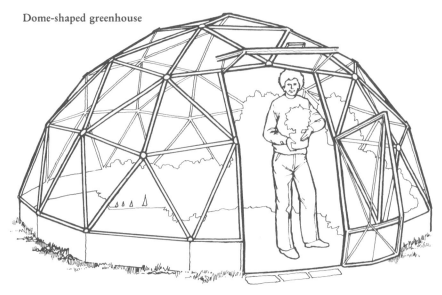

Dome-shaped

Although it may look like something from outer space this geodesic dome is roomy, exceptionally well lit and very strongly made. Triangular panes of glass cover the entire structure but the bottom half may be fitted with solid panels to give a half-timbered effect. Several of the panes are hinged to allow ventilation, and the panel above the door lifts to allow tall gardeners (or short ones carrying tall plants) plenty of headroom.

Available only in aluminium.

Lean-to

As an extension to your house, as well as your garden, a lean-to greenhouse offers many advantages. It insulates the house wall, the central heating system may be used to heat it, it is easily accessible in wet weather and can be positioned on walls of any aspect. Shelves can be attached to the back wall (which is best painted white to improve the light intensity) and both half-timbered and glass-to-ground models are available.

If you are particularly short of space consider a miniature lean-to. On a patio or balcony this type of structure is small enough and light enough to fit the bill. It can be positioned over a window and even suspended so that its base is off the floor. The sliding door allows access but not entry. As a little plant raiser it is very useful, but if positioned in full sun it will heat up very rapidly. For this reason site it on an east-, west-, or north-facing wall, or use it to grow plants that do not object to

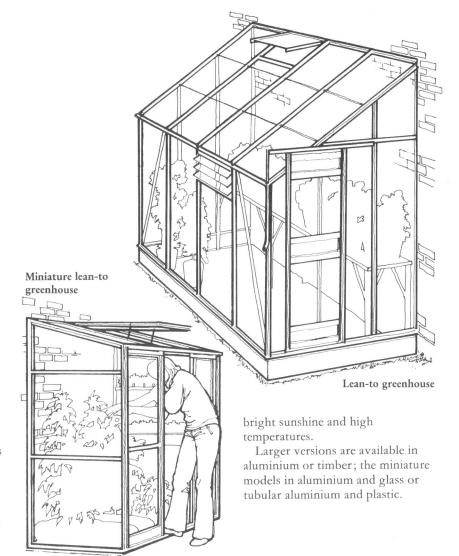

Lean-to greenhouse

Miniature lean-to greenhouse

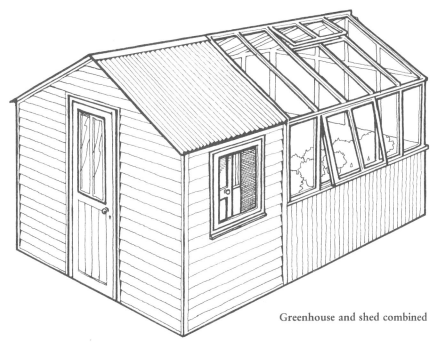

bright sunshine and high temperatures.

Larger versions are available in aluminium or timber; the miniature models in aluminium and glass or tubular aluminium and plastic.

Greenhouse and shed combined

The gardener/handyman may consider this to be the greenhouse of his dreams! A potting bench, bins of compost, plant pots and tools can all be stored in the timbered half which acts as a separate workroom or potting shed. The other section takes the form of a span-roofed greenhouse (though models are available with a lean-to greenhouse attached to the side of a shed) and the two are linked by a door. The door to the outside world is set in the shed portion so entrances and exits need not affect the greenhouse temperature.

Available in timber.

Greenhouse and shed combined

Types of greenhouse

Uneven span

Unlike the span-roofed greenhouse, the uneven span has sides and roof panels which may be of different sizes and which slope at different angles. The design shown here allows large plants such as tomatoes to be cultivated on the highest side, while pot plants set on shelves and staging can be grown opposite. To make the best use of available light the largest side should face south. Do make sure that the uneven span greenhouse you choose has adequate ventilation facilities – particularly at the apex of the roof.

Models are available in timber and aluminium. The greenhouse shown here is constructed of timber and rigid corrugated plastic – a covering which will last from five to ten years before it needs to be replaced.

Uneven-span, corrugated plastic greenhouse

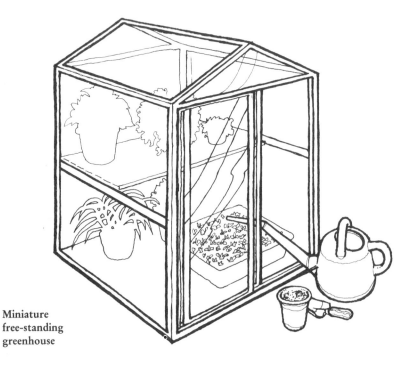

Miniature free-standing greenhouse

Miniature

Although you cannot actually get inside this greenhouse it does offer a fair amount of space for raising bedding plants and early vegetable crops. It is light, portable and needs no foundations so is well suited to being used on patios and roofs. There are several designs available – the one shown here has a rigid span-type roof and sliding glass doors to allow ventilation and access. Miniature free-standing greenhouses should always be positioned in a very sheltered spot; they are not anchored and so need protection from strong winds. In summer you will find that the air inside this greenhouse heats up extremely quickly, so move it to a slightly shady part of your patio or roof to keep the temperature down. Available in aluminium.

Plastic tunnel

A polythene greenhouse is well worth having if you lack the permanent site or funds necessary for a glazed structure. A sturdy tubular steel or aluminium framework supports a one-piece polythene 'envelope' whose margin is buried in the ground for anchorage and stability. No foundations are necessary and the greenhouse can be uprooted and moved around the garden as you wish to cover fruit or vegetable crops which are to be forced. Alternatively the structure may be used in the same way as a permanent greenhouse and equipped with staging to hold pot plants. The two door panels – one at either end – are the only means of ventilation and these may open on hinges or slide up and down on nylon cord. The polythene envelope will have to be renewed every two years or so.

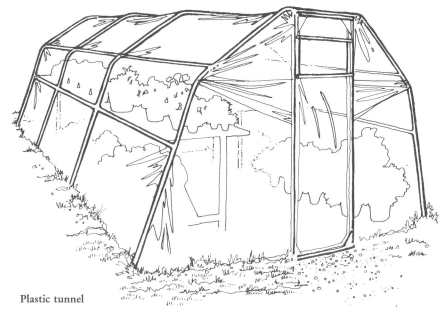

Plastic tunnel

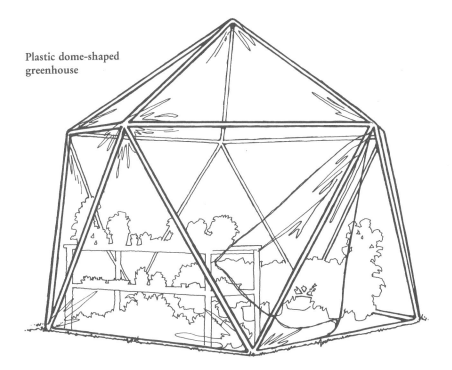

Plastic dome-shaped greenhouse

Plastic dome

If you want a polythene greenhouse with a more eye-catching design than a tunnel choose a dome. The tubular aluminium framework is staked to the ground to give it stability and, again, a polythene envelope fits over it. Ventilation this time is by means of one opening in the roof and a large triangular facet of the house which folds back and also acts as the door. Like its longer counterpart, the dome can be moved around or positioned in one place and equipped with staging. Replacement envelopes are available.

With both this design and the tunnel I would strongly advise you to view an erected model of the type you intend to buy so you can see just how strong – or weak – it is going to be. Polythene greenhouses vary tremendously in quality.

Foundations and construction

Unless you have decided on a polythene structure your greenhouse is going to need permanent foundations to hold it level and to prevent rot or corrosion from destroying the base.

Ready-made bases

Many manufacturers will supply ready-made bases to fit their greenhouses. If one is available for the model you choose pay the extra charge and save some hard work.

Two kinds of base are usually offered: those made of precast concrete and those made of steel. The concrete type comes in the form of precast kerbs which are slotted together to make the required shape. Bolts are used to hold the greenhouse firmly to its instant footings. In very sheltered gardens the weight of the base may be sufficient to anchor the greenhouse, but in gardens exposed to wind the corner sections should be bedded in concrete.

Steel bases usually come in four long sections which are bolted together at the corners. They will support the greenhouse well but are not weighty enough to hold it down. For this reason the corners of steel bases should always be bedded in concrete or bolted to steel stakes driven into the ground.

Whether you lay precast concrete or steel foundations the following precautions should be taken:

1 Lay the foundations in a 5-cm (2-in) deep trench whose base has been firmed and levelled.

2 Check the kerbs or steel sections with a large wooden set-square to make sure that the corners are right angles.

3 Check all four sides with a spirit level to make sure they are laid evenly.

4 Set the corners in concrete where necessary.

Home-made foundations

If the greenhouse of your choice is not supplied with foundations you will have to build some yourself. The job is a fiddly one but quite within the scope of anyone who can wield a spade or knock a nail into a piece of wood.

1 Use four garden canes to mark out the area to be occupied by the greenhouse and check that the corners are right angles by using a large, wooden set-square. Make sure that you allow room to walk around the greenhouse if it is positioned near a wall or fence.

2 Take out a trench the depth and width of a spade blade and half fill it with rammed rubble. Position one brick at either end of each side and adjust them until they are level, checking frequently with a spirit level and a straight edge. These bricks indicate the height of the finished concrete foundation and so all eight of them must be at the same level.

3 Mix 1 part cement with 6 parts all-in ballast and add water until the final mixture is of a moist but firm consistency. Deposit the mixture on top of the rammed rubble and tamp it down evenly with a wooden straight edge to the level of the bricks.

4 Once the concrete is dry a single row of bricks can be cemented into position to hold the greenhouse clear of the ground. Mix 1 part cement with 4 parts sand and add water to make a mixture of a spreadable consistency. Lay a brick at each corner first (checking their positions with the set-square) and lay the rest against string drawn tightly between two of the originals. Use a spirit level to check that the bricks are laid evenly.

5 To make sure that the greenhouse will be held firmly to its footings sink metal coach-bolts into the cement between the bricks every yard or so. Alternatively, metal 'L'-shaped brackets can be laid under the bricks with one side protruding vertically. These will be fastened to the base of the house once it is in place.

Precast concrete foundations

Building foundations:
1 Bricks are used to create a level base;
2 Tamping down concrete to make it absolutely smooth;
3 Laying a damp-proof course.

6 When the cement is dry the greenhouse can be erected. First, place a layer of roofing felt over the bricks to act as a damp-proof course.

Erecting the greenhouse

If you've managed so far on your own you will now need another pair of hands to help you. A sectional wooden greenhouse is erected as follows: Place the plain end of the greenhouse on the foundations and bolt first one long side and then the other to it. The door section can then be bolted into place and all four sides checked to see that they are sitting properly on the brick base. Drill any holes necessary to take the coach bolts from the foundations.

The two roof sections can now be slid into place and individually bolted on. Fix the ridge capping to the apex of the house and attach any ventilators supplied separately. Finally, secure the base of the greenhouse to the coach bolts or metal brackets.

If, for one reason or another, you are not able to put up your own greenhouse, buy from a manufacturer who offers a free erection service.

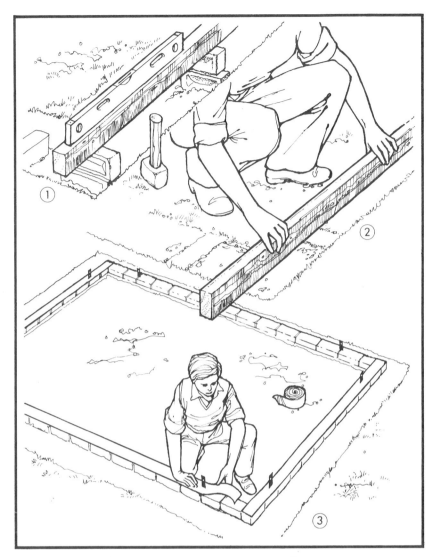

The final stage of construction: sliding on the roof panels.

Glazing

Unless the manufacturer supplies your greenhouse with the glass already in place it should be glazed after it has been erected and not before. Horticultural grade glass – usually referred to as 3 mm or 24 oz – is the type to use and should be supplied cut to size by the greenhouse manufacturer.

Aluminium greenhouses can be glazed with great speed because the glass is held in position by plastic strips and snap-on or screw-on metal clips. The traditional wooden house may have grooves into which the glass can slide, or it may rely on putty and glazing sprigs to hold the glass in place. Don't be put off a greenhouse which has all the right features just because it sounds messy to glaze. Follow these instructions and the job is made simple:

1 Take some putty out of its container and knead it in your hand until it is reasonably soft. Check that the glazing bars of the greenhouse are clean and feed the putty on to the rebate with your thumb. Putty two facing rebates of the greenhouse at a time so that you can glaze an entire strip, working from bottom to top to allow the glass to overlap.

2 Place the bottom piece of glass in position and press down on each edge with your fingers so that the glass beds firmly in the putty.

3 Secure the glass with glazing sprigs tapped in horizontally at either side of each pane. Four are usually sufficient to hold one piece of glass in place. Position further panes of glass above the lowest one, allowing a 1 cm ($\frac{1}{2}$ in) overlap each time. When these panes are in position and held down with sprigs, tap in one sprig at either side under the lower edge of each pane to prevent it slipping down. The lowest panes on the roof can be

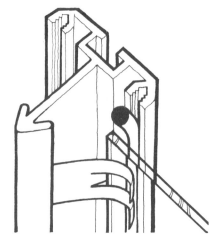

On aluminium houses putty is not necessary; the glass is held in place by means of strong clips.

held up with one sprig tapped vertically into the wooden rail that runs the length of the greenhouse.

4 With a knife, old wood chisel or screwdriver, clean off the surplus putty and knead it in your hand to use on the next strip.

5 Wipe the glass immediately inside and out with a damp cloth to remove any putty marks; if left to dry they are extremely difficult to get off. Glaze the roof first and then the sides of the house, endeavouring, if possible, to complete the job in one day. A half-glazed greenhouse can be badly damaged by wind.

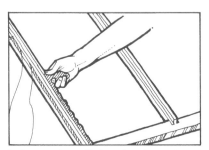

Soft putty is applied to the glazing bars.

The glass is pressed into position.

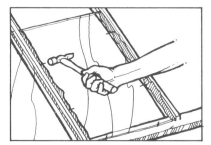

Sprigs are tapped into place to secure the glass.

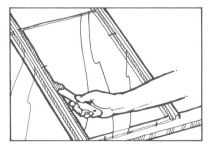

Extra putty is scraped off with a sharp knife.

1 Bubble polythene
2 Roller blinds
3 Ventilator
4 Paraffin heater
5 Potting compost
6 Mains tap
7 Electric control panel
8 Louvre ventilator
9 Soil border
10 Capillary watering unit
11 Slatted staging
12 Electric propagating unit
13 Concrete slab path
14 Thermometer
15 Extra shelving unit

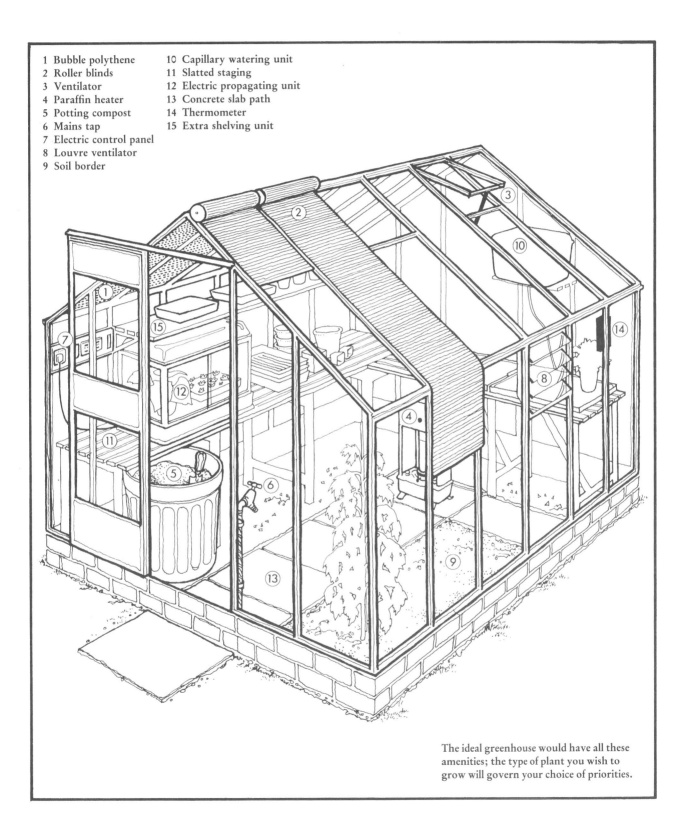

The ideal greenhouse would have all these amenities; the type of plant you wish to grow will govern your choice of priorities.

Heating

To get the most out of your greenhouse some kind of heating is essential, even if it is only used in spring to give flower and vegetable seedlings an early start. If you can afford to provide a little heat from November to March you can beat the frosts, keep tender plants such as geraniums going and produce a good range of winter-flowering pot plants to brighten the darker months of the year. As you can see, the amount of heat you need to give depends on the plants you want to grow, so decide what you will require from your heater before you go out and buy. Of the many different heating systems available those shown on the following pages are the most useful.

Paraffin Heaters

For the greenhouse gardener who just wants to boost his temperatures in spring the paraffin heater is a good choice. It is relatively inexpensive to buy and although the fuel is fairly expensive it goes a long way.

Good points
– Requires no connection to mains services and so can be used in isolated greenhouses.
– Gives off carbon dioxide which the plants can use.
– Can be fitted with hollow or water-filled extension pipes to assist heat distribution.
– Can be used to boost other heating systems.
– Easily portable.
– Can be connected to a larger supply tank to make filling less frequent.

Bad points
– Can give off damaging fumes which will burn foliage.
– Creates excessive humidity and condensation – the water trays supplied seldom need to be used.

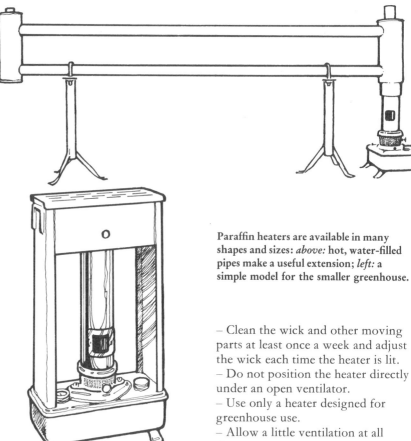

Paraffin heaters are available in many shapes and sizes: *above:* hot, water-filled pipes make a useful extension; *left:* a simple model for the smaller greenhouse.

– Cannot be thermostatically controlled.
– Fuel has to be stored.
– Heater must be attended to regularly.

For best results
– Choose a heater large enough for your greenhouse (manufacturers will always advise) and one which is well made.
– Use only the best quality paraffin.
– Stand the heater on a firm and level base where air can circulate around it.
– Keep the heater out of draughts.
– Choose a blue-flame type which gives off less fumes than the yellow-flame burners.

– Clean the wick and other moving parts at least once a week and adjust the wick each time the heater is lit.
– Do not position the heater directly under an open ventilator.
– Use only a heater designed for greenhouse use.
– Allow a little ventilation at all times.
– Clean the heater and store in a dry place when it is not in use.

Electric heaters

There are several types of electric greenhouse heater, all of which are very efficient and very effective. Tubular radiators can be fixed to the sides of the greenhouse (underneath staging if it is present) and the heat they give off will rise and circulate. Fan heaters should be positioned on the greenhouse path and directed so that the warm air they blow out does not come into direct contact with plants and cause scorching. Air-warming cables can be fitted to the inside of small greenhouses such as miniature lean-tos and will give off sufficient heat to keep out frost (larger heaters would be too powerful). They are also useful if buried in the medium contained in a propagating case where they will encourage cuttings to root more rapidly. They have the advantage that they are much cheaper to run than fan or tubular heaters.

Good points
– Can be thermostatically controlled and so keep temperatures even and avoid expensive wastage.
– Gives out dry heat which discourages moisture-loving fungus diseases in winter.
– Clean and fumeless.
– Keeps air circulating.
– No fuel storage necessary.
– Automatic and therefore labour saving.

Bad points
– Relatively expensive to run.
– Requires mains supply which must be specially laid on.
– Possibility of power cuts.

For best results
– Choose a heater large enough for your greenhouse (manufacturers will advise) and one which is well made.
– Adjust the thermostat to give maximum economy and efficiency.

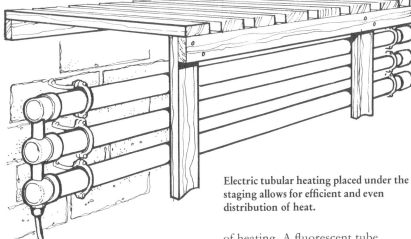

Electric tubular heating placed under the staging allows for efficient and even distribution of heat.

– Position the unit where its heat will be well distributed.
– Use only electric heaters, plugs and accessories designed for greenhouse use.
– Clean and store fan heaters in a dry place when not in use and have them checked over by an electrician once a year.

Electricity
A supply of electricty in your greenhouse will be of great value whether or not you use it as a means of heating. A fluorescent tube attached to the ridge of the house allows plants to be tended to on dark winter evenings, and a heated propagating case will make the rooting of cuttings and the raising of seedlings much easier.

If you do decide to equip your greenhouse with electricity consult an electrician first and arrange for him to connect up the supply and fit the power points. He will advise on the correct kind of fittings and will also know the regulations that apply when laying cables underground or running them overhead. Where two or more power points are required a control box can be fitted inside the greenhouse so that all the switches are in one place. The box may also incorporate a mains on/off switch and all the controls will be housed in a strong protective casing. One final word: never use household electrical fittings in a greenhouse – they are not designed for use where humidity is high and water may be splashed around.

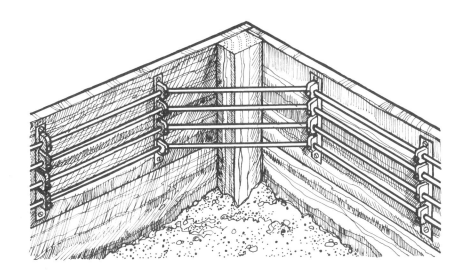

Electric air-warming cables can be used to heat a small space such as a garden frame or miniature greenhouse.

Heating

Gas heaters

Since the introduction of natural gas, greenhouse heaters which use this fuel have become very popular. Coal gas was often a problem to indoor gardeners because its fumes scorched the leaves and flowers of house plants. Natural gas is much cleaner and can be used with safety in a greenhouse which contains a range of flowers, fruit and vegetable crops.

Natural gas heaters can usually be adapted to run on bottled propane if it is not possible to connect them to the mains, though running costs will be considerably higher with this fuel.

Like electricity, the gas supply should be connected by a professional fitter who will advise on the pipes and equipment necessary.

Good points
– Can be thermostatically controlled to ensure economy.
– Needs little maintenance.
– Relatively cheap to run.
– Gives off carbon dioxide which the plants can use.
– No fuel storage necessary (if natural gas is used).
– Automatic and therefore labour saving.
– Usually fitted with a safety cut-out.
– Can be fitted with hollow pipes to aid heat distribution.
– Pilot light can be allowed to burn all the year round to give carbon dioxide enrichment.

Bad points
–Requires mains supply which will have to be specially laid on (unless bottled propane is used).
– Creates high level of humidity which can encourage fungus diseases in winter.
– Running costs are high for propane-burning models.
– Propane must be transported and stored.

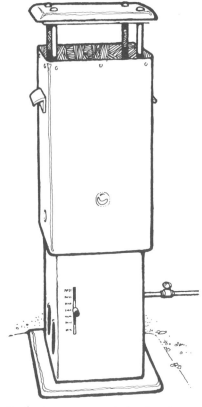

Gas heaters are economical and can be run on mains or bottled gas.

For best results
– Choose a heater which is large enough for your greenhouse (manufacturers will always advise), and one which is well made.
– Stand the heater on a firm and level base where air can circulate around it.
– Keep the heater out of draughts.
– Allow a little ventilation at all times.
– Adjust the thermostat to give maximum economy and efficiency.
– Position the unit where its heat will be well distributed; fit extension pipes if necessary.
– Do not position the heater directly under an open ventilator.
– Keep the air inlets unobstructed at all times.

– Check the pilot light at daily intervals and clean the choke system when necessary.

Boilers

For larger greenhouses which are over 3 m (10 ft) wide and 4.5 m (15 ft) long, solid-fuel, gas- or oil-fired boilers connected to water-filled pipes provide a worthwhile and reliable means of heating. The initial outlay is high and the unit is bulky but it will provide plenty of clean, dry heat.

The boiler should be positioned outside the greenhouse (preferably at the door end) under some kind of protective cover to shelter it from the elements. The pipes will run from the back of the boiler around the inside perimeter of the greenhouse and may be 5–10 cm (2–4 in) in diameter.

Good points
– Clean and fumeless pipe system inside the greenhouse.
– Gives out dry heat which does not encourage moisture-loving fungus diseases.
– Good heat distribution.
– Relatively slow cooling down if boiler goes out.
– Can be thermostatically controlled.

Bad points
– Slow to respond when quick increase or decrease in temperature is required.
– Bulky.
– Cannot be used very effectively in small greenhouses.
– Corrosion can be a problem.
– Solid fuel or oil has to be stored.
– Needs daily stoking and routine cleaning.
– Expensive to buy and relatively time-consuming to install.
– Ashes have to be disposed of.
– Boiler and chimney can be unsightly.

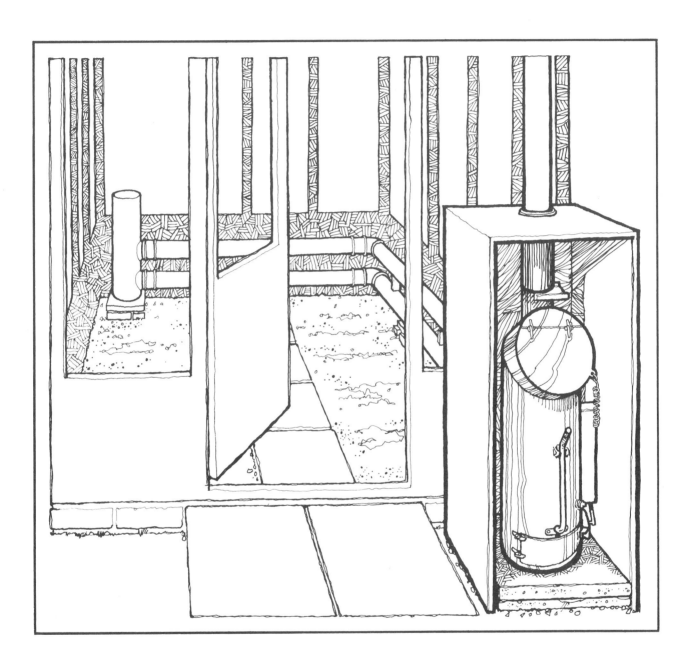

For best results
– Choose a heater which is the right size for your greenhouse (manufacturers will always advise) and one which is well made.
– Adjust the thermostat to give maximum economy and efficiency and the damper to control fuel burning.

– Use only the fuel recommended by the manufacturer.
– Provide some form of protective housing for the boiler but leave the front open to allow in air.
– Attend to stoking and cleaning as recommended by the manufacturer.
– Install this type of heating only in larger greenhouses.

A boiler with hot pipes is expensive to install but an efficient way of providing heat.

Temperature control

To ensure that your plants are healthy and your money is not wasted you will have to discover how to control the temperature in your greenhouse. In winter, ways of conserving heat must be found, and in summer the air must be kept cool.

Heat conservation

Once your greenhouse is equipped with a heater your first priority is to make sure that as little heat escapes as possible. The most obvious way to do this is to check that doors and ventilators fit tightly and do not admit cold draughts. Site the heater where its warmth will be well distributed and keep the greenhouse glass as clean as possible so that full use is made of the sun.

From November to March it is worth fitting insulation material to the inside of greenhouses heated to a temperature of 10°C (50°F) or more. Some greenhouse manufacturers sell insulating panels tailored to fit the lower part of their glass-to-ground greenhouses as these lose more heat than half-timbered types. Polythene is a suitable alternative if you want to insulate the roof sections as well. Fasten the lining to the framework of the greenhouse so that a 1–2.5-cm ($\frac{1}{2}$–1-in) layer of air is trapped between the polythene and the glass, but take care to attach a separate piece of polythene to each ventilator so that it can still be opened when necessary. 'Bubble' polythene is more effective but slightly more expensive: the air trapped in it gives additional insulation. Drawing pins will hold the material to the inside of a wooden house – adhesive tape and ingenuity will have to be used where aluminium is concerned.

If you feel that it is unnecessary to insulate your entire greenhouse, drape a curtain of polythene from the roof so that it partitions off one side or an end of the house and position the heater there to make a warm corner. Avoid making the compartment totally sealed – the heater and plants should have some air circulating around them.

Thermostats

Many electric greenhouse heaters are supplied with built-in thermostats. If this is not the case then you must arrange for a thermostat to be wired into the circuit. Apart from saving money by turning the heater off when it is not required, it will benefit the plants by maintaining an even temperature.

There are several types of thermostat, the most popular being the type which consists of a temperature-sensitive rod. A rod thermostat can be used to monitor greenhouse air temperatures and may also be fitted to a propagating case, but make sure that it is specifically designed for greenhouse use. An electrician will advise you on how it can be connected to your heating system.

Ventilation

In summer your problem will not be how to conserve heat but how to dissipate it. Even in a short spell of bright sunshine a greenhouse will heat up rapidly, and unless something is done to lower the temperature your plants will roast. If you choose a greenhouse with enough ventilators to allow a good circulation of air you will have few problems. One ridge and one side ventilator for every 2 m (6 ft) of the greenhouse's length is the general requirement, but the more there are the better. Ventilators on both sides of the house will always allow you

Bubble plastic provides temporary insulation over the winter months.

to admit air on the leeward side.

The traditional ventilator consists of a hinged window which can be opened to varying degrees with a casement stay. Today louvred vents are very popular and frequently fitted to aluminium greenhouses. They have a tendency to be less tight-fitting than ordinary ventilators so make sure that they do not admit draughts in winter. On the good side, louvre units can be used to replace ordinary panes of glass, allowing you the option of having as many extra ventilators as you can afford. In the height of summer the door of the greenhouse and all the ventilators can usually be left wide open during the day, provided there is no wind.

Automatic ventilation

If you invest in only one piece of automatic equipment for your greenhouse, make it an automatic ventilating arm. These units are now widely available, reasonably priced and act as a reliable safety valve if you have to leave your greenhouse unattended all day.

Each unit is powered by a slim cylinder filled with petroleum jelly which expands as temperatures rise, forcing up a lever which opens the vent. As the air cools, so the jelly contracts and the vent is lowered. No external power source is used and the unit can be pre-set to open a ventilator at the required temperature from 13°C (55°F). Automatic arms can be fitted to one or all of your ridge and side ventilators.

Fans

As an optional extra in your greenhouse, a small roof-mounted circulating fan will keep the atmosphere gently moving, so avoiding a build-up of hot air. Extractor fans are more practical still and can be fitted to the end of the house opposite the door to create a through-flow of cooling air.

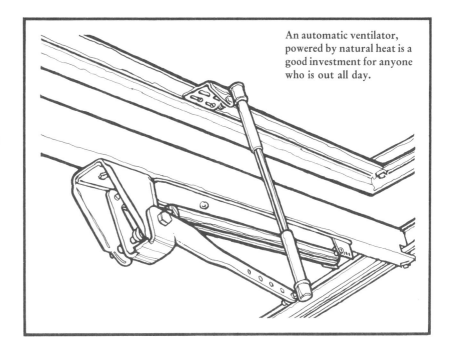

An automatic ventilator, powered by natural heat is a good investment for anyone who is out all day.

Fasten down the louvres of extractor fans with adhesive tape in winter to keep out draughts.

Thermometers

No greenhouse should be without a thermometer. The ordinary type is useful as far as it goes, but you should really invest in a maximum and minimum thermometer if you want to know what happens in your greenhouse when you are not there. This type of thermometer has two mercury columns, equipped with little metal needles which are pushed by the mercury and remain in position indicating the highest and lowest temperatures reached in the preceding twenty-four hours. The needles can be re-set each morning with a magnet or a push button. Take a note of your thermometer's readings and adjust your heating and ventilation accordingly. For accurate readings the thermometer should be hung out of direct sunlight in a place where air can circulate around it.

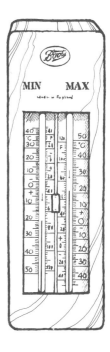

A maximum and minimum thermometer is an essential for any greenhouse.

Shading

Protecting plants under glass from the direct glare of scorching sun is just as important as ensuring that they have a good supply of cool air. To prevent leaves and flowers from being burnt at the edges some form of shading will have to be provided on the south- and west-facing sides of the greenhouse in summer.

There are several products available for use in and on the greenhouse to stop your plants suffering from sunburn: here are some of the most effective.

Shading compounds

By far the cheapest method of shading plants, these compounds come in powder or liquid form and are mixed with water to make whitewash of varying intensity which is applied to the outside of the glass with a brush or spray. 'Coolglass' clings electrostatically to glass and no amount of rain will shift it. In the autumn, though, it can be wiped off easily with a dry duster. It also has the advantage of

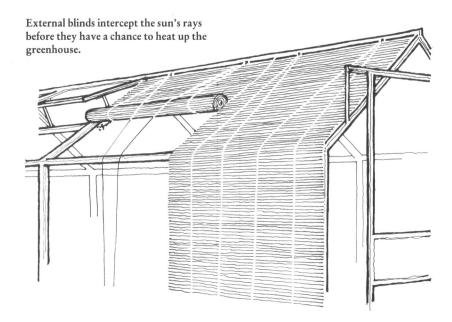

External blinds intercept the sun's rays before they have a chance to heat up the greenhouse.

being suitable for use on polythene greenhouses.

Another product, 'Vari-shade', is white when dry and translucent when wet, so allowing more light to pass through the glass on rainy days. Always paint shading

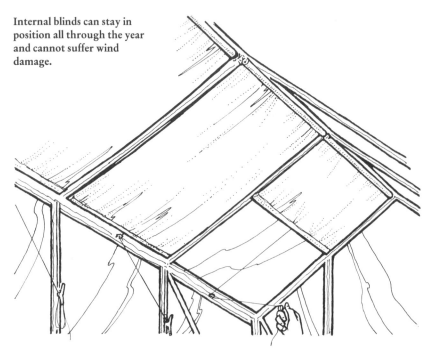

Internal blinds can stay in position all through the year and cannot suffer wind damage.

compounds on to the glass of cedar greenhouses very carefully so that the wood is not stained.

Blinds

The best greenhouse blinds are those fitted to the outside of the house so that they intercept the sun before it has a chance to heat up the air inside. External blinds made of plastic strips, bamboo canes and wooden laths are readily available but they might cost more than you are prepared to pay. However, if they are stored carefully when not in use (in a dry garage or shed) they will last for many years. Always check that external blinds do not impede ventilation.

Internal blinds are not to be completely shunned for they do cut down unwanted glare and the ventilators can be easily operated when they are in position. They may be made of plastic or linen and fitted to spring rollers for easy retraction. The great advantage of all blinds is that they can be rolled up on dull summer days.

Scrim or muslin

If you don't want the bother of having to paint on shading, but you can't afford blinds, settle for the happy medium with a roll of coarse muslin or scrim which can be attached to the inside of the house and held in position with drawing pins (if the house is made of timber) or adhesive tape (if the house is made of aluminium). Rolls of this material can be obtained quite cheaply and cut to fit your greenhouse.

It is argued, quite sensibly, that shading material should be as light coloured as possible so that light is reflected rather than absorbed. Dark green material cuts down glare but is less effective at keeping down temperatures than its white equivalent, even though it does look more pleasing in the garden.

When should you shade?

At any time from late April the sun may come out in sharp bursts that could damage seedlings and shade-loving plants. Internal blinds can be pulled down and raised at will all the year round, but external ones must be rigged up in late April to early May and taken down and stored in late September.

Shading compounds can be applied to the glass from late May onwards, and before this protect sensitive plants with sheets of newspaper in hot spells.

Remove all shading in mid- to late September. As the sun gets weaker and lower the plants will need all the light they can get.

Scrim or muslin makes a cheap and effective form of shading but once in position cannot easily be removed on overcast days.

Paths and borders

Whether your greenhouse is equipped with staging to support plants, or soil borders in which they are planted direct, some sort of pathway will almost certainly be needed down the centre of the house. Trampled soil is unsatisfactory since it will leave your shoes muddy, allow weed seeds to germinate and be generally unhygienic. One of the following surfaces will be clean, effective and cheaply installed.

Gravel

Purchased from your local builders' merchant, washed pea shingle is surprisingly cheap and just a few sackfuls will be sufficient to provide a 5- to 8-cm (2- to 3-in) layer on the floor of the average greenhouse. The shingle will prevent weeds from emerging and can be soaked with water to provide a more humid atmosphere when required (this operation is known as damping down). Spread the shingle on the path area and underneath the staging too if plants are not to be grown in the soil. An occasional rake over will keep it evenly distributed.

Concrete slabs

If you want a narrow path down the centre of the house, precast concrete slabs are easily laid on a bed of sand to provide a firm walkway. They can be damped down in the same way as gravel and easily swept clean.

Damping down the path of the greenhouse helps to keep the temperature down and maintain a humid atmosphere.

Duckboarding

As an alternative to gravel and concrete slabs, slatted duckboarding can be made quite simply from 2.5 by 8 cm (1 by 3 in) timber. Several sections 60 cm (2 ft) or so wide may be laid end to end down the centre of the greenhouse. Weeds will have to be removed if they emerge through the boards but you can damp down and still walk around without getting your feet wet.

Soil borders

If your greenhouse is built on good land there is no reason why you should not plant tomatoes, chrysanthemums, vines, peaches and

Border soil should be enriched each year by the addition of organic compost.

The problem of poor or infected border soil can be overcome by using ring culture.

other tall crops directly into the existing border soil. Some experts recommend removing the soil to a spade's depth at the outset, lining the trench with polythene and filling it with John Innes compost. I have always considered this to be an expensive waste of time unless the soil in the border is known to be poor or contaminated.

If the existing soil is reasonable, work in a bucketful of very well rotted garden compost or manure and 55 g (2 oz) of a general fertilizer such as Growmore or blood, bone and fish meal per running metre or yard, and give the border a good soak with the hosepipe the day before planting. Provided that you vary the crops you grow in the border each year, and add more enrichment, then you can look forward to years of good service from your soil. Only when the

plants show signs of being unhappy do you need to go to the length of digging out the soil and replacing it.

If you intend to grow only tomatoes in your greenhouse border there is an alternative to planting them in the soil. A 15-cm (6-in) layer of washed pea shingle or gravel can be laid over the border and retained with wooden boards. Instead of being planted in the border soil the tomatoes are grown in bottomless pots or 'rings' placed on the shingle. The feeding roots will stay in the soil provided in the rings and the drinking roots will penetrate the shingle to which all water is applied. Well-weathered ashes can be used in place of shingle but avoid peat since it can become sour and stunt the plants' growth.

The shingle or ash can be washed through with a hose each winter and used for many years.

Staging and shelving

To grow pot plants comfortably and well you will need some kind of staging on which they can stand. Set at waist height, or just below, the staging can run right down one side of your greenhouse or all the way round it if you prefer. The width will be governed by the distance between the door and the side of the greenhouse, but bear in mind that 1 m (3 ft) is the maximum distance over which you can comfortably lean.

There are several types of staging available. Many manufacturers offer wooden or aluminium benches tailored to fit their own greenhouses; if you can afford them they are usually well made. Always look for stability and strength: pots and boxes full of compost weigh a lot when grouped together, and flimsy benches will buckle and collapse under the strain.

Aluminium

Aluminium staging is usually constructed with two layers of solid gravel trays or with wire or plastic netting which allows air to circulate around the plants. The humidity provided by gravel is not always wanted in winter when moisture-loving fungus diseases can be a problem, so open benching is preferable at that time of the year. Alternatively, gravel can be placed in shallow plastic trays which are removed and stored in winter or just left dry.

If you use the lower shelf of the staging not for shade-loving plants but for storing pots, make sure that you wash them first and cover them with a sheet of polythene to keep them clean.

Always allow a small gap between solid staging and the side wall of the

Aluminium staging

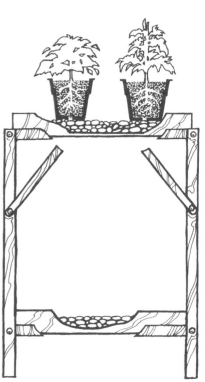

Tiered wooden staging allows the maximum number of plants to be on display.

When the staging is put in position in the greenhouse make sure that it has a firm footing. If the floor underneath it is not solid stand each leg on a brick sunk into the soil. Wooden staging can be screwed to the sides of a wooden house to give it extra stability.

Shelves

When you have used what seems like every available inch for staging, don't forget that you can probably put up a few shelves too, even if

only on a temporary basis. They do cut down light but can give valuable room for bedding plants and vegetable seedlings in spring. Narrow shelves can be supported by inverted 'L'-shaped brackets 23 cm (9 in) or so below the eaves of the house, and wider shelves slung on 'U'-shaped brackets under the ridge. If the shelves can be easily dismantled they can be removed to let in more light as soon as the temporary greenhouse occupants are moved out.

A shelf slung from the ridge of the greenhouse and a narrow shelf on a bracket alleviate a shortage of space.

greenhouse so that air and heat can circulate well.

Wooden staging

If you can wield a hammer and screwdriver with reasonable proficiency, try making your own slatted wooden staging from 5 by 2.5 cm (2 by 1 in) timber. Deal is suitable and can be coated with preservative to prolong its life. The legs can be made from 5 cm (2 in) square timber and should be positioned at 1.5 m (5 ft) intervals. Tiered staging on three different levels really makes the most of all available space and is well worth constructing on benches 1 m (3 ft) wide.

Watering

Of all the skills at a gardener's elbow, watering must certainly rank as one of the most important. To beginners it seems a complex art that is difficult to master, so let's take a look at the secrets of success.

When to water

As a general rule, a plant should be watered when the compost in the pot is dry. Keep the compost constantly moist and trouble will be the result; let it stay dry for several days and the leaves and flowers will droop and eventually turn crisp and brown.

There are only one or two exceptions to the general rule: plants such as azaleas, ferns and insectivorous plants like to be kept constantly moist; cacti and other succulents store water in their leaves and stems and can do without it in the soil for several weeks. But with most pot plants overwatering will cause wilting from which the plant will not recover; plants wilting because of dryness at the roots can usually be revived.

Here are a few tests you can make to check whether or not a pot plant is dry:

1 Look at the surface of the compost and feel it with your fingers. It may occasionally dry out when the soil in the rest of the pot is moist but it usually a good guide.

2 Lift the pot plant and compare its weight with one known to be moist. If it is dry it will feel considerably lighter.

3 Sound clay pots containing dry compost will ring when tapped with a wooden cotton reel fixed to the end of a bamboo cane. If the compost is moist only a dull thud will be heard. Cracked pots of course will never ring.

4 If you have no intention of mastering the skills of watering, or if you are a born coward, invest in one of the proprietary moisture-testing meters available. Flashing lights, little arrows or intermittent bleeps will let you know whether the soil is wet or dry.

5 When dealing with soil in beds and borders the state of the surface is no guide at all. Dig down 10 or 15 cm (4 or 6 in) with a trowel to see if the soil is moist.

How to water

When a plant is found to be dry, give it a good drink: pour water on to the surface of the compost until it reaches the rim of the pot, then allow it to soak into the compost. You will see the importance of leaving an adequate gap between the surface of the compost and the rim of the pot: as a rough guide, 2.5 cm (1 in) of water will be sufficient to moisten 23 cm (9 in) of compost.

Plants that produce a dense rosette of leaves which cannot be penetrated by the watering can may be watered from below. Provide each of these plants with a saucer which can be filled with water and emptied of any surplus half an hour later.

Finally, remember never to water by the clock; plants drink when they are dry, so in sunny weather they will need watering more frequently than on dull, cold days.

The water supply

To save time and effort try to arrange for an alkathene supply pipe to be laid to the greenhouse. The pipe should be buried 60 cm (2 ft) deep in the soil to prevent it from freezing up in winter. A plumber will advise on the quality of pipe needed and will connect it to the mains for you.

Alternatively, if your greenhouse is fitted with guttering and downpipes you can invest in a waterbutt or, better still, take the downpipes inside the greenhouse and lead them to a large tank sunk in the ground below the staging. One foot from a pair of tights can be fastened over the end of the pipe to prevent debris from being deposited in the tank. The advantage of tank water is that it is not icy

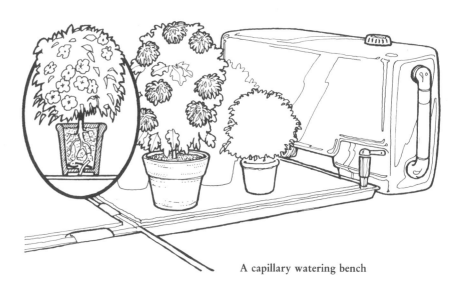

A capillary watering bench

cold in winter, but great care should be taken to prevent compost and leaves from falling in the water or disease may result.

Watering cans

The good old watering can is the simplest piece of watering equipment and one of the most efficient. The type known as the Haws model is the easiest to use in the greenhouse; it has a long spout which will allow you to reach plants at the back of the staging without knocking over those at the front. It can also be fitted with sprinkler heads or 'roses' for watering seedlings and newly potted plants without disturbing the soil. You will find that a one-gallon can is the most convenient to carry in a small space.

Hosepipes

Connected to the greenhouse tap the hosepipe will save a lot of time and effort when watering. One word of warning: use it at a slow trickle and don't be tempted to turn it on too fast or the compost will be washed out of the pots. Lance attachments fitted with on/off triggers are available and these can be attached to the end of the hose for greater control. Use the watering can fitted with a rose where seedlings are concerned.

Capillary watering

Some people argue that automatic watering takes away half the fun of greenhouse gardening, but it is very useful at holiday times and if you are out all day.

Years ago the only capillary benches available were bulky objects covered in a layer of sand that had to be replaced when it became dirty. Now simple units are manufactured which make use of

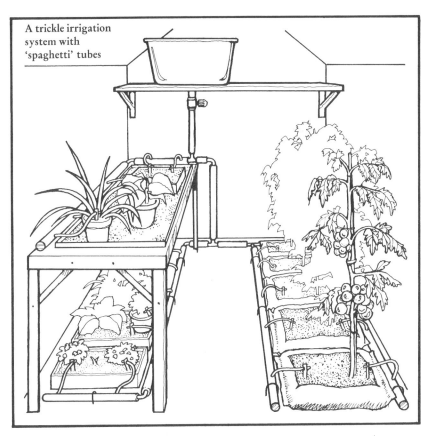

A trickle irrigation system with 'spaghetti' tubes

shallow plastic trays fitted with plastic fibre matting. The trays are supplied with water by a neat, plastic tank and the fibre draws up the water by capillary action. Pot plants standing on the matting will take up the right amount of water, just when they need it.

Plastic pots are the best type to use on capillary benches for they have an abundance of holes in the base which allow the compost to come into contact with the matting. Clay pots can be used but the crocks must be left out at potting time. Instead a strip of the plastic fibre is drawn through the hole to act as a wick. When the matting becomes coated with green algae it can either be boiled clean or treated with an algicide.

Capillary units are valuable in summer but can offer too much

water to plants in the winter months. The plastic type I have mentioned can easily be cleaned and stored when not in use.

Trickle irrigation

A length of alkathene piping supplied by the main and equipped with a multitude of spaghetti-like small-bore tubes is another popular type of automatic watering system. Each spaghetti tube is held over a pot with a little plastic support and when the water supply is turned on, every plant at the end of a tube is watered. Although this system saves much time it is not selective and some plants are bound to be given too much or too little water. However, it will be found to be very useful where a large number of plants are being grown.

Composts

Plants growing in the garden have an endless supply of soil at their disposal. Pot plants, on the other hand, have relatively little compost from which to feed so we must make sure that the mixture is richer than ordinary soil and that it offers everything the plant will need. Swift drainage, adequate moisture retention and a supply of essential nutrients are the main features of a good compost.

The old gardeners considered that each plant needed a different mixture especially formulated to cater for its whims and fancies. Fortunately research has proved otherwise and a limited range of excellent composts can now be used to grow a wide range of plants to perfection.

John Innes composts

The most popular composts are undoubtedly those in the John Innes range. The formulae for these seed and potting composts were developed back in the 1930s by Mr Lawrence and Mr Newell – two members of staff at the John Innes Horticultural Institution, and composts described as 'John Innes' are now offered by many manufacturers. To be sure of buying J.I. compost which is made to the original specifications look for the seal of the John Innes Manufacturers' Association on the bag. There are a lot of J.I. composts about that bear no resemblance to the real thing.

Adventurous gardeners can make their own John Innes composts by following these original formulae.

Loam

For best results the loam used in these mixtures should really be derived from a stack constructed of turves which have been allowed to break down. Good garden soil, provided that it is neither too heavy nor too light, is a fair substitute. It

---

John Innes No 1 potting compost (JIP1)
7 parts by volume partially sterilized loam
3 parts by volume granulated peat
2 parts by volume coarse sand
+
4 oz John Innes base fertilizer
$\frac{3}{4}$ oz ground limestone or chalk $\Big\}$ *to each bushel*
Use: Pot up newly rooted cuttings and prick out bedding plants and seedling pot plants in this mixture.

John Innes No 2 potting compost (JIP2)
(same basic ingredients)
+
8 oz John Innes base fertilizer
$1\frac{1}{2}$ oz ground limestone or chalk $\Big\}$ *to each bushel*
Use: Grow most pot plants in this mixture.

John Innes No 3 potting compost (JIP3)
(same basic ingredients)
+
12 oz John Innes base fertilizer
$2\frac{1}{4}$ oz ground limestone or chalk $\Big\}$ *to each bushel*
Use: Grow tomatoes, cucumbers, melons, chrysanthemums and other large and vigorous plants in this mixture.

John Innes Ericaceous compost
(same basic ingredients)
+
4 oz John Innes base fertilizer   *to each bushel*
Use: Grow azaleas, rhododendrons, heathers and other lime haters in this mixture.

John Innes seed-sowing compost
2 parts by volume partially sterilized loam
1 part by volume granulated peat
1 part by volume coarse sand
+
$1\frac{1}{2}$ oz superphosphate of lime
$\frac{3}{4}$ oz ground limestone or chalk $\Big\}$ *per bushel*
Use: Sow all seeds in this mixture.

should be sterilized in a proprietary electric soil sterilizer at 65°C (180°F) for 10 minutes to kill weed seeds and damaging pests and diseases. It may also be sterilized in the following way if an electric sterilizer is not available: Boil about $\frac{1}{2}$ in water in a large saucepan, fill the pan to the brim with dry soil which has been passed through a 1-cm ($\frac{1}{2}$-in) sieve and simmer for a quarter of an hour. Then tip out the soil and allow it to cool.

Peat

Ordinary granulated peat (the type supplied in bales) should be broken down and passed through a 1-cm ($\frac{1}{2}$-in) sieve before use. It should be moist rather than dry but is not easy to mix when very wet.

Sand

Coarse river sand is the type to use – not bright yellow builders' sand which contains impurities, or silver sand which is too fine.

Bushel measure

A bushel measure can be easily made at home. Construct a box 25 cm by 25 cm by 55 cm (10 in by 10 in by 22 in); full to the brim it will contain one bushel.

Fertilizers

The fertilizers mentioned should be available from any good garden centre or hardware shop. John Innes base fertilizer can be made at home if you wish. It consists of a mixture of:

   2 parts by weight hoof and horn
   2 parts by weight superphosphate of lime
   1 part by weight sulphate of potash.

Mixing

When the ingredients have been measured out and sieved where necessary, spread them out to make a flat-topped heap and turn this three or four times with a shovel

Mix your own John Innes compost using the 'recipes' opposite.

until the compost looks an even colour.

Storing

Avoid storing the compost for longer than you have to. Two months is usually given as a maximum amount of time; after this the compost may start to turn sour. Plastic sacks or dustbins will keep the mixture clean and moist.

Cutting compost

Many recipes are given for compost used to root cuttings, but I find that a mixture of coarse river sand and granulated peat in equal parts is very effective in producing roots on a wide range of plants.

Soilless composts

Many proprietary composts are offered for sale nowadays and most of them contain no soil at all. They consist mainly of peat, to which nutrients and maybe a little sand

have been added. They are light, clean and easy to use, but the plants will exhaust them of nutrients more quickly and so will have to be fed regularly about six weeks after being potted. If soilless compost is allowed to become too dry, heavy plants may overbalance.

When you use soilless compost remember the following tips:

1 Try not to let the compost dry out completely or it may be difficult to moisten again.

2 Do not firm the compost too much when potting – push it lightly into place with your fingertips.

3 Do not place crocks in clay pots if soilless compost is being used – compaction and bad drainage are unlikely.

4 Store the compost in a cool, dark place so that it remains moist.

5 Avoid potting very large plants in a soilless mix.

Containers

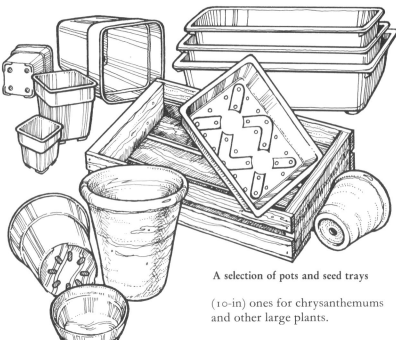

A selection of pots and seed trays

There is an enormous range of plant containers available. Before you buy, sort out which ones are likely to be the most useful for your particular needs.

Clay pots

Good to look at and heavy enough to anchor plants well, clay pots are the favourites of many gardeners. However, they do need to be crocked (this involves placing pieces of broken clay pots in their bases to prevent the single hole from becoming blocked) and they will almost certainly break if dropped on a hard surface. They also have a tendency to become coated with green algae but this can easily be scrubbed off. Soak new clay pots in water overnight before use or they will absorb too much water from the compost. Like plastic pots they come in a variety of sizes but you will find 8-, 10-, 12-, and 20-cm (3-, 4-, 5-, and 8-in) diameter pots the most useful, with a few 25-cm

(10-in) ones for chrysanthemums and other large plants.

Plastic pots

These are now manufactured in far greater quantity than clay pots and so are more readily available. They are light, less fragile and easier to keep clean than their clay counterparts. Plastic pots have several holes in their bases so crocks are not needed, and they are more suitable than clay pots for use on capillary benches. The fact that plastic pots are not porous means that visits with the watering can should be slightly less frequent.

Plastic pots are available in a greater variety of shapes and colours than clay pots. Choose the type you like the look of but make sure that the plastic is not too thin.

Half-pots are available in clay and plastic. These have the same rim diameter as ordinary pots but are only half as deep. They are fine for dwarf bulbs, alpines and other plants with shallow root systems.

Polythene bags

Black polythene bag-pots are

extremely cheap and ideal for raising the larger bedding plants which are potted individually. Perforations in the base ensure good drainage. The bags are removed before planting and can be washed and used again.

Peat pots

Where lettuces, broad beans and other crops are being raised under glass, peat pots make highly suitable containers because they can be left on at planting time, so avoiding major root disturbance. When planted up the pots will hold together best if they are grouped in seed trays or boxes, and they should always be kept moist. A good soak at planting time will make sure that the plant's roots can penetrate the pot and reach the soil.

Seed trays

These may be plastic or wooden. The former, being easy to clean and store, have largely replaced the older wooden variety, although these may sometimes be obtained very cheaply from fruit or fish dealers. In spite of their shortcomings they do not crack like plastic ones if they are lifted unevenly. Contrary to popular opinion seed trays do not need a layer of crocks or roughage in the base. Plastic trays have lots of small drainage holes and can be filled direct with compost; wooden trays can be lined with a sheet of newspaper to prevent compost from falling through the cracks. For seedlings and bedding plants, trays 8 cm (3 in) deep will be suitable.

Rings

Tomatoes being grown on the ring culture system are best planted in rings which are 23 cm (9 in) in diameter. These may consist of plastic pots with their bottoms removed, or specially made rings of aluminium or whalehide (a type of bituminised paper) may be bought from horticultural sundriesmen. Discard whalehide rings at the end of the season; the others may be cleaned and used again.

Growing bags

The growing bag is one of the simplest and most labour-saving plant containers. All it consists of is a polythene sack of soilless compost which is laid flat on the ground. Holes are made in the top, the compost is soaked with water and tomatoes, cucumbers etc. may be planted, or sown, in the compost. Excellent yields can be obtained from crops raised in growing bags, and they are especially useful where

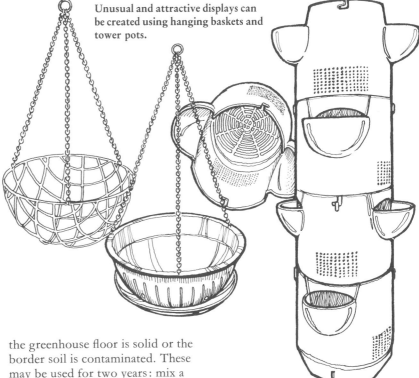

Unusual and attractive displays can be created using hanging baskets and tower pots.

Tomatoes grown on the ring culture system showing details of the roots

the greenhouse floor is solid or the border soil is contaminated. These may be used for two years: mix a little fertilizer with the compost and grow a less demanding crop such as lettuce in the second season.

Hanging baskets

To see trailing plants to best effect, grow them in hanging baskets. These are lined with black polythene or sphagnum moss, filled with compost and planted up. Bedding plants can be used in outdoor baskets in summer, and trailing greenhouse plants can be grown in them all the year round under glass. It is also possible to buy plastic 'baskets' with built in drip-trays. Hanging baskets dry out very quickly in warm weather so check them for water at least once a day.

Troughs

Either as windowboxes or extensions to the greenhouse staging, troughs make another good home for compact or trailing plants. Small

plastic troughs can be slung from the front of the staging; larger types may be stood on the floors of conservatories and moved outdoors in summer.

Tower pots

These tall pots take up very little floor space but can accommodate a surprising number of plants. Each section of the tower has two pockets in which trailers or bushy plants may be grown, and when established the whole unit turns into a tower of flowers and foliage. Water is applied to each pocket and any surplus makes its way down the tower through the system of drainage holes in the base of each section. As well as being suitable for pot plants, tower pots are also useful for strawberries. The fruits are kept clean and can be brought to early maturity when grown in a greenhouse.

Propagation

Propagators

Raising your own plants is one of the greatest pleasures of greenhouse gardening. Not only will you feel a sense of achievement at producing a plant from a seed or a cutting but you will also save money. A warm, humid environment is what most seeds and cuttings prefer in their early days of development, and you can provide this by making or buying a small propagating case or frame.

A home-made propagating frame

To build yourself a simple propagating frame all you need is about 3.2 m (10 ft) of 20-cm (8-in) by 2.5-cm (1-in) timber. This can be sawn into four lengths and screwed together to form a rectangular box 60 cm (2 ft) by 1 m (3 ft). Position this firmly on your greenhouse staging and lay a piece of asbestos or sheet metal under the frame if the staging is slatted.

Cuttings root best if they are supplied with 'bottom heat', and if your greenhouse is equipped with electricity this can be provided by fitting soil-warming cables to the propagating frame. First spread a 5-cm (2-in) layer of moist sand in the base of the frame and then lay the special soil-warming cable on this, running it back and forth across the sand in even loops. Manufacturers of soil-warming cables will give an indication of how much is needed to heat a given area. If all your cuttings and seeds will be raised in pots and boxes the cables can be covered with a 5-cm (2-in) layer of sand on which the containers will rest. If cuttings are to be dibbed directly into the frame then a 10-cm (4-in) layer of peat and sand mixed together in equal parts should be spread over the cables. To keep the air around the young plants warm a few circuits of cable may be attached to the frame above the level of the medium.

For maximum economy, and to

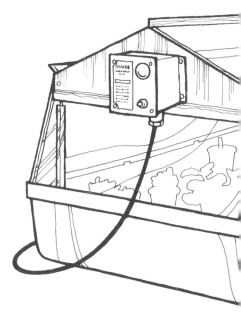

A large glass propagating unit, fitted with thermostat

keep the frame at an even temperature of 16–18°C (60–65°F) a rod thermostat should be fixed to the frame and wired into the system. The element should protrude among the pots and boxes if plants are being raised in containers, but it should be covered by the layer of peat and sand if cuttings are being rooted direct in the medium.

All this heat will quickly disperse unless some kind of cover is provided to maintain a close atmosphere. Rig up some wire hoops and spread a cover of thin polythene over them to keep the air around the seeds and cuttings warm and moist. Remove and shake the polythene each day to clear it of any condensation that might have collected, and allow a little ventilation at all times.

Keep the sand or the rooting medium moist at all times. This will make sure that the heat is effectively conducted and that the plants' roots do not dry out.

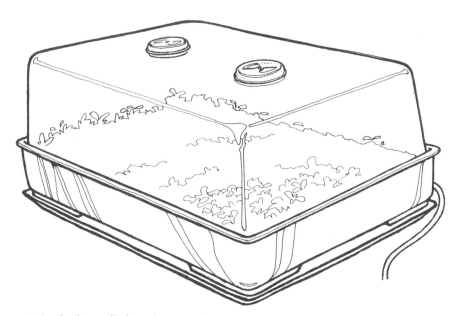

A simple, electrically-heated propagating tray

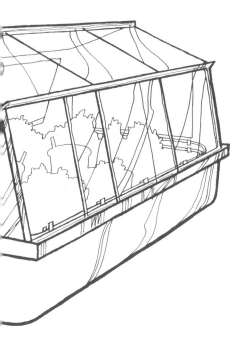

panel above the burner. Again, these propagators are not thermostatically controlled but they do provide the essential warmth.

If all you can afford is a few perspex-covered trays, stand them on the staging directly above your existing greenhouse heater – you'll still get fair results.

The most expensive propagator is the electrically heated model with a strong, moulded plastic base and a built-in thermostat. The glass cover admits more light than its plastic counterparts and is fitted with sliding doors for easy access.

Mist propagation

Some cuttings are difficult to root in an ordinary propagating frame, but they will often establish themselves more quickly if sprayed at intervals with water. The mist propagating unit is an automatic system of doing this. An 'electronic leaf' (which consists of two electrodes embedded in plastic) is positioned among the cuttings and connected, via a system of valves and wires, to an atomiser which is positioned overhead. When the electronic leaf is wet the circuit is made and the unit remains inactive. When the water evaporates the circuit is broken and a fine mist is sprayed over the cuttings until, once more, the electronic leaf is evenly coated with water. By keeping the cuttings moist the system reduces water loss and speeds up rooting.

A mist unit can be attached to any heated propagating frame of sufficient size, but a polythene screen should be positioned around it to avoid moisture loss and stop you getting wet. Kits are available which contain all the necessary equipment.

Shop-bought propagators

If you lack the time or inclination to make your own propagating frame there are many versions offered by manufacturers at prices to suit all pockets.

The cheapest consists of an electrically heated grid over which sits a plastic seed tray covered with a perspex hood. This unit is not thermostatically controlled but it uses relatively little electricity and is therefore quite economical. The plastic hood is usually fitted with two swivel ventilators to allow in air. The tray and grid combine to make a good propagator for gardeners who raise only a few plants from seeds and cuttings, both of which are inserted directly in seed or cutting compost which fills the tray.

The same perspex-covered seed trays can be used even if your greenhouse is not supplied with electricity. Some small paraffin heaters are specially adapted to support two or more trays on a

A mist propagation unit

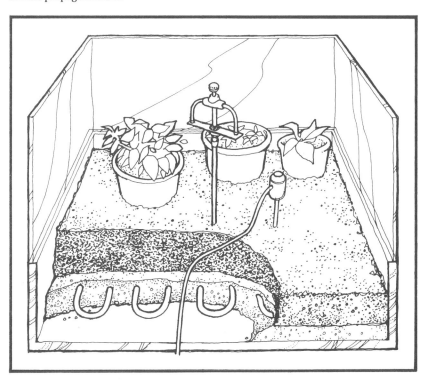

Propagation

Seed propagation

A packet of seeds represents superb value for money. For just a few pence you can buy the makings of a large crop of flowers, fruits or vegetables – all you need to do is provide the conditions necessary to force them into growth.

To make sure you get the best results from your seeds remember the following tips:

1 Buy from a reputable seedsman whose stock will germinate well and be true to name. Order early to avoid disappointment.

2 Never be afraid to try new varieties, but also ask your friends to recommend their old favourites.

3 Store your seeds in a cool, dark, dry place. Kept in an airtight container they will remain fresh for a long time.

4 Try to use fresh seed each time you sow, though seed of flowers and vegetables will often retain its viability for a number of years if stored well (see the charts opposite).

5 Sow the seeds at the right time of year and under the right conditions. Moisture, air and the correct temperature are all important.

Seed packets

Most seedsmen take great care to provide plenty of information on their seed packets about the germination and subsequent cultivation of the young plants. Always read the information before you sow and, if possible, act on it.

The best seed packets are those which are hermetically sealed. These keep the seeds as fresh as possible, so prolonging their life. The sealed packet may be large and carry printed instructions, or it may be quite small and contained in a more colourful paper envelope. Whichever is the case, do not open the sealed packet until you intend to sow.

Storage life of vegetable seeds

Seed	Years	Seed	Years
Aubergine	5	Marrow	5–6
Beans	3	Melon	5
Beetroot	4	Onion	1–2
Broccoli	5	Parsley	1–3
Brussels sprouts	5	Parsnip	1–2
Cabbage	4–5	Pea	3
Carrot	3–4	Pepper	4
Cauliflower	4–5	Pumpkin	4
Celeriac	5	Radish	5
Celery	5–6	Salsify	2
Chicory	5	Scorzonera	2
Chinese cabbage	5	Seakale	1–2
Corn salad	5	Spinach	5
Cucumber	5–6	Squash	5
Endive	5	Sweet corn	1–2
Kale	5	Swiss chard	4
Kohlrabi	5	Tomato	4
Leek	3	Turnip	5
Lettuce	4–5		

Storage life of flower seeds

Seed	Years	Seed	Years
Ageratum	4	Hibiscus	3–4
Alyssum	3	Impatiens	2
Antirrhinum	3–4	Kochia	2
Aster	2–3	Lobelia	3–4
Browallia	2–3	Marigold (African & French)	3–4
Calendula	3–4	Mesembryanthemum	3–4
Campanula	3	Mignonette	2–4
Candytuft	3	Mimosa	2–3
Carnation	3–4	Nasturtium	3–4
Celosia	4	Nemesia	2–3
Cineraria	3–4	Nicotiana	3–4
Clarkia	2–3	Nigella	2
Cobaea	2	Pansy	2–3
Coleus	2	Petunia	3–4
Cosmos	3	Polyanthus	2
Cyclamen	3–4	Primula	2
Dahlia	2–3	Salpiglossis	4–5
Delphinium	2	Salvia	2
Dianthus	3	Schizanthus	2–3
Eschscholzia	2	Stocks	4–5
Gaillardia	2	Sweet pea	3–4
Godetia	3	Verbena	2–3
Gomphrena	2–3	Wallflower	5
Gourds	5–6	Zinnia	3
Heliotrope	1–2		

1 Fill the seed tray with compost.

2 Gently firm the soil at the edge of the tray with the fingertips.

3 Firm the soil using a home-made presser in a seed tray or the base of a smaller pot if a pot is being used.

F₁ hybrids

Seeds which are described as being F_1 hybrids are usually more expensive than the run-of-the-mill kinds but are well worth the extra cost. They will give rise to sturdy high-yielding plants of great vigour and robust health. F_1 hybrids are produced by crossing two specially selected plants, and while the seeds you sow will produce a uniform crop, any seeds saved from these plants will give rise to varied and inferior offspring. For this reason the seedsman has to cross-pollinate each year to produce the hybrid seeds and this is why they are more costly.

Pelleted seeds

Seeds of more popular varieties of vegetables and bedding plants are often offered in pelleted form, each being surrounded by a type of clay (which may contain a fungicide), thus making spacing much easier. Pelleted lettuce seed, for instance, can be more effectively spaced out in the row than ordinary seeds; antirrhinums can be space-sown in boxes so that pricking out is made unnecessary (though liquid feed will have to be applied to keep the young plants healthy).

The thing to remember about all seeds is that they must never be allowed to dry out after sowing. With pelleted seeds this rule is particularly important, for the slightest suspicion of dryness often results in complete failure. As pelleted seeds are much more expensive than untreated ones you will have to consider whether the convenience outweighs the cost.

Special treatment

There are just a few seeds which will not germinate readily if sown in the normal way. Sweet peas, for instance, have a hard seedcoat which can make germination very slow, and for best results they should be

chipped with a knife on the side opposite the scar. Other hard-coated seeds can be soaked for a few hours to soften them.

Whereas most seeds germinate best in the dark, some are known to do better if kept in the light. Among these are cacti and succulents, calceolarias, ficus species, gloxinias, lettuce, nicotianas, petunias, primulas, saintpaulias and streptocarpus.

If in doubt, consult the seed packet which should offer helpful guidance.

Preparing to sow

Most seeds will germinate well if sown in trays or pots of good seed compost such as John Innes or a soilless equivalent. Don't sow a great boxful of seeds if you only need a few plants – sow them in a pot. Make sure that the compost is moist at sowing time and work on a clean, firm surface.

Seed trays are filled in the following way:

1 Overfill the tray with compost, making sure that it is spread right out to the corners.

2 Lightly firm the compost with your fingertips making sure that there are no large air pockets at the edges or in the corners of the tray.

3 Take a short piece of board and scrape off any excess compost.

4 Firm the surface of the compost with a home-made presser to leave it 1 cm ($\frac{1}{2}$ in) below the rim of the container and so allow for watering.

5 Pots are filled in a similar manner and the compost is simply firmed by using the base of another pot.

If the compost in pots and boxes is further moistened at this stage you will be able to avoid watering and disturbing the seeds immediately afterwards. Soak the containers using a watering can fitted with a fine rose, or stand them in a shallow tray of water until the compost has taken up sufficient moisture.

Propagation

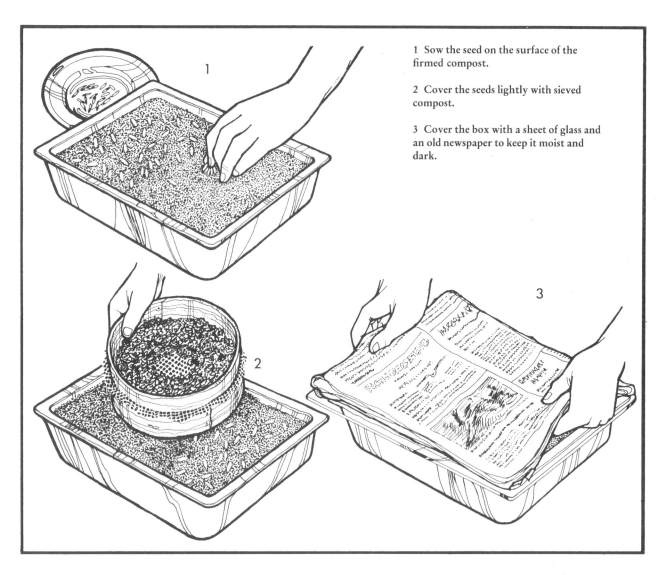

1 Sow the seed on the surface of the firmed compost.

2 Cover the seeds lightly with sieved compost.

3 Cover the box with a sheet of glass and an old newspaper to keep it moist and dark.

Sowing the seeds

When the compost in your containers has been thoroughly moistened it is ready to take the seeds. Most can be sown directly from the packet – take a pinch in your fingers and scatter it evenly over the surface of the compost so that it is thinly distributed. Most seeds should then be given a light covering of compost applied through a 0.5-cm (¼-in) sieve. Stop sieving as soon as the seeds can no longer be seen.

Very small seeds such as begonias, calceolarias, lobelia and streptocarpus need no covering at all. It is very difficult to sow dust-fine seeds evenly and for this reason they can be mixed in the packet with a little fine sand before being scattered over the compost. The light-coloured sand will show up well on the dark surface to give you an indication of how evenly the seed is being distributed.

Large seeds such as broad beans, marrows and melons can be sown individually in peat pots and planted out pot and all when they are large enough. As a rough guide, larger seeds should be covered to 1½ times their own depth.

As soon as you have sown each container, label it clearly to show the variety and the date on which it was sown. Place the containers in a propagating frame or over the greenhouse heater (a temperature of 16–18°C (60–65°F) is adequate for most seeds) and cover them first with a sheet of glass and then with newspaper. These coverings help to keep the seeds warm and moist.

Check the boxes and pots every day to see if germination has taken place and wipe the glass clean of any condensation. When the first seedling appears in any box or pot, remove the glass and paper and stand the container in a well-lit part of the greenhouse.

When the compost starts to dry out, water it very carefully with a can fitted with a fine rose. A little Cheshunt compound may be mixed with the water. This preparation will guard against damping off – collapse of the seedlings caused by a fungus disease. On very sunny days prevent the seedlings from being scorched by covering them with single sheets of newspaper.

Pricking out

When the seedlings are large enough to handle they may be pricked out into seed trays or small pots of John Innes No 1 potting compost or a soilless equivalent. Most bedding plants and vegetable seedlings will

Pricking out seedlings

Single seeds may be sown in peat pots.

go in the trays, larger bedding plants such as salvias, stocks, heliotrope and any plants which are to be grown in containers all their lives are pricked out singly in 8-cm (3-in) pots.

Use a pointed dibber or a pencil to transfer the seedlings and always handle them by their first pair of leaves, not by the stems. Space seedlings 4 to 5 cm ($1\frac{1}{2}$ to 2 in) apart in boxes. Approximately 35 seedlings (5×7) will fit in a standard plastic seed tray. Lift a few seedlings from their seed tray and gently tease their roots apart. Make a hole in the compost in the new tray for each seedling, lower it into place and firm the compost around its roots.

Label each tray as it is completed and water the seedlings into their new home with a watering can equipped with a fine rose.

Very small seedlings such as begonias can be pricked out with a sharp-pointed stick. Prise them from the compost and gently bed them into the surface of the compost in their new container. Lobelia is best pricked out in little clumps when it is quite small.

Shelter all newly transplanted seedlings from bright sunshine for a few days and continue to water at intervals with diluted Cheshunt compound.

Propagation

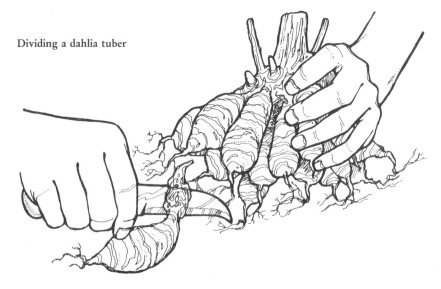

Dividing a dahlia tuber

Not all plants set seeds, and some that do produce inferior offspring. For this reason other means of increase have to be used. Those on the following pages are the most popular.

Division
Clump-forming pot plants are very easy to propagate. Most of them have a fibrous root system and all you need to do is knock the plant from its pot, tease the roots apart and pull the clump into several pieces which have a good supply of roots and shoots. Tougher plants may have to be cut apart with a knife.

Pot up the new plants individually in John Innes No 1 potting compost or a soilless equivalent. Division is best carried out in spring, for the plants will grow away quickly in the warm weather that follows.

Dahlias can also be propagated by division. The tubers are normally stored in dry peat or sand during the winter months to protect them from frost. In spring they can be brought into the gentle warmth of the greenhouse and placed in a mixture of moist peat and sand. As soon as shoots start to form, remove the tubers from the peat/sand mix and

divide them with a sharp knife. Each new plant must have a tuber and at least one shoot. Pot up these divisions individually and grow them on for planting out in early summer. Plants raised in this way will often perform much better than those left undivided.

Plantlets
At times Nature really does her best to help the gardener, and plants which produce instant scaled down versions of themselves are one of her best ideas.

The spider plant (chlorophytum) carries its young on the end of long stems. Peg these plantlets into pots of compost and sever them as soon as they have rooted, or allow them to rest in jars of water until roots form before cutting them off and potting them up. The mother-of-thousands dangles her offspring on hair-thin stems in a similar way and these, too, can be removed and potted up.

The succulent bryophyllum produces tiny new plants in the serrations of each leaf – when they are ready to lead a life of their own they drop off and take root. Before this happens gently pull them off

and sit them on the surface of small pots of moist compost. They will soon grow away rapidly.

All plantlets may be rooted and removed from the parent plants at any time of year.

Layering
Trailing plants such as ivy and philodendron produce very long stems which can be propagated by layering. Push the central part of the stem to be layered into a box or pot of compost, and hold it below the surface with a loop of wire. Soon roots will emerge from the buried portion of stem and the new plant will grow away. Cut it from the parent plant as soon as it is established.

Air layering
When greenhouse plants outgrow their allotted space, or their stems become bare and ugly, don't think that all you can do is throw them on

Chlorophytum plantlets can easily be rooted in soil or water.

Air layering a rubber plant
1 An upwards cut is made into the stem at an angle of 45°.
2 The incision is filled with sphagnum moss.
3 This is then wrapped in a further layer of moss and finally polythene which is sealed with tape.
4 When roots have formed the new plant is severed from the stem and potted up.

Ivy may be propagated by layering.

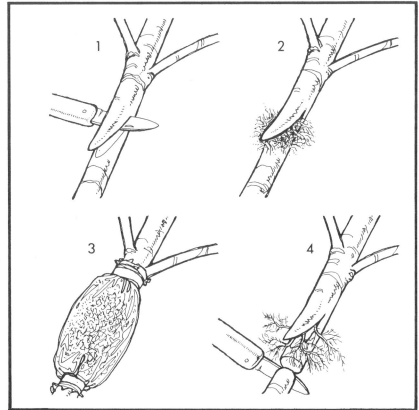

the compost heap. Many can be propagated by air layering and several new plants obtained from the old one.

Make an upward incision a few inches below the lowest remaining leaf, or nearer to the shoot tip if you need a smaller plant, to leave a cut about 4 cm (1½ in) long at an angle of 45°.

Fill the incision with moist sphagnum moss or coarse peat and work a band of the same material around the stem. Wrap a 10-cm (4-in) wide strip of polythene around the moss or peat and seal it top and bottom with adhesive tape or twine. Prevent the stem from snapping by using a short length of bamboo cane as a splint.

Rooting may take several weeks or several months depending on the greenhouse temperature. Aim for 21°C (70°F) if you want speedy results. When you can see plenty of root activity underneath the polythene, undo the ties and sever the upper part of the plant. Potted up in good compost and cossetted in a warm part of the greenhouse for a few weeks it shouldn't look back. Even the old plant may take on a new lease of life if you cut it back to buds which may be forced into growth.

Propagation

Propagation by cuttings

Cuttings provide a means of propagation for a large number of plants. They may be made from stems, leaves and even roots. The plant section at the back of the book gives details of the best method of propagation for each species.

Softwood cuttings

These are taken while growth is young and fleshy; with shrubs this will be in spring or early summer,

Left: The cutting is taken from a healthy plant.
Above: The cutting is dipped into hormone rooting powder and then inserted into the growing medium.

but plants such as pelargoniums and coleus retain a good number of soft young shoots until late in the season.

Remove healthy young shoots from the plants you want to propagate, cutting off the required stems just above a leaf joint, or node, so that no unsightly stalk is left behind. Prepare the cuttings for insertion by removing the lower leaves and making a clean, straight cut below a leaf joint with either a very sharp knife or a razor blade. The finished cutting should be 5 or 8 cm (2 or 3 in) long (though pelargoniums may be up to 10 cm (4 in) long).

Some cuttings (e.g. Busy Lizzie and tradescantia) are easy to root in jam jars of water. Place the jars where you can keep an eye on them and pot up the cuttings when they have made about 2.5 cm (1 in) of

root. If the roots grow any longer they will be damaged at potting time.

Most cuttings should be rooted either in a propagating frame or in pots of cutting compost. Dip the stem base in hormone rooting powder, tap off the excess and dib in four cuttings around the edge of a 10 cm (4 in) pot, or in greater numbers in rows in the propagating frame. Half the stem should be buried in the medium.

If only a small number of cuttings are to be taken you may like to use a rooting bag. These miniature growing bags contain a peat-based compost and the cuttings are inserted through slits made in the upper surface. The bags give extremely good results – particularly with pelargoniums.

Always label the cuttings clearly when they have been inserted and

water them in. A propagating frame should be covered with a sheet of polythene, single pots can be topped with polythene bags fastened in place with an elastic band.

Pelargoniums have rather hairy leaves and are best not covered as they tend to rot if the atmosphere is kept too humid. Most cuttings will root well in a temperature of 16–18°C (60–65°F). Shelter them from scorching sunshine with single sheets of newspaper.

When roots have formed the cuttings will start to grow and can then be potted up individually.

Half-ripe cuttings

From July onwards the shoots on many plants begin to harden and they are then described as being half-ripe. Most shrubby garden plants are propagated from half-ripe cuttings and the method of preparation is just the same as for softwood cuttings, except that these firmer ones may be an inch or so longer. Some shrubs root more readily if the cuttings are torn from the parent plant with a 'heel' or piece of woody stem. The heel is trimmed and the cutting inserted in the usual way. Once rooted the cuttings can be potted up and overwintered in the garden frame before being planted out in spring.

Leaf cuttings

There are a few plants that can be propagated by rooting portions of their leaves. Amongst these are African violets (saintpaulias), Cape Primrose (streptocarpus) and *Begonia rex*.

The large leaves of *Begonia rex* can be laid on a moist bed of sand (or sand and peat) and the main veins slit with a knife. Hold the leaf down with one or two pebbles and keep the rooting medium moist. An occasional spray over with water will keep the leaf fresh. New plants will appear where the slits are

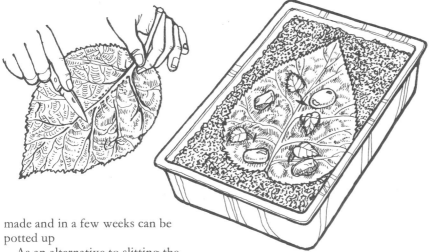

Plantlets can be grown from slit veins on the leaf of *Begonia rex*.

made and in a few weeks can be potted up

As an alternative to slitting the veins the leaf may be cut into squares slightly larger than a postage stamp and these are dibbed vertically into the compost for half their length. Take care to insert them the right way up (with the sap flow running from base to tip). When new plants arise from the base of each cutting pot them up.

African violets (saintpaulias) are propagated using a leaf and its stalk. Remove suitable healthy leaves and insert them so that the stalks are completely buried in a propagating frame or pot of cutting compost. Keep them in a humid atmosphere and soon a new plant will emerge at the base of each leaf.

Cape primrose (streptocarpus) has long, narrow leaves which can be cut into sections and dibbed into the rooting medium. Make sure that the sections of leaf are the right way up and a new plant will arise at each central vein.

Root cuttings
Quite a few herbaceous plants and one or two vegetables can be raised from root cuttings which are very easy to prepare. Anchusa, hollyhock, horseradish, seakale, oriental poppy, verbascum and romneyas all have

thick roots. Dig the plants up in winter, cut off pencil-thick sections of root about 5 cm (2 in) long and make sure you keep them the right way up: make a straight cut at the top and a sloping one at the bottom to prevent mix-ups. Dib the cuttings into trays of cutting compost so that they are just buried, and place the trays in an unheated frame or greenhouse for the winter. In spring shoots will be produced and the new plants may be set out in beds, borders or rows.

More fibrous-rooted plants such as phlox and gaillardia may also be propagated from root cuttings. Trim the roots into 5-cm (2-in) lengths and scatter these over the surface of some cutting compost in a seed tray. Sieve 1 cm ($\frac{1}{2}$ in) of compost over them and treat them in the same way as their thicker counterparts.

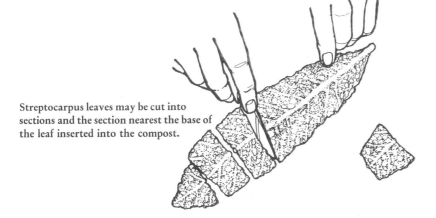

Streptocarpus leaves may be cut into sections and the section nearest the base of the leaf inserted into the compost.

Potting and planting

However carefully you choose containers and compost for your plants they may perform very poorly if you pot or plant them in a slap-dash way. Take your time and do the job properly – you will enjoy the job more and so will the plants.

Potting

All plants grown in containers have to be moved from time to time. The first potting of a rooted cutting or seedling is known as 'potting up'. Any subsequent moves into larger pots are described as 'potting on'. Very occasionally it is not necessary to give a plant a larger container but some fresh compost is beneficial. In this situation the plant is knocked from its pot, some of the old compost teased away and the plant

Potting up: the seedling is transplanted from the seed tray to its first pot.

Potting on: a plant is transplanted into a bigger pot to give it room to develop.

put back in its original container with a little fresh compost. This is known as 're-potting'.

Spring and summer are the best times of year to undertake any form of potting, for then plants are growing freely and will soon become established in their new homes.

The method of potting depends on the container and the compost used, but make sure that the pots are clean and that the plants to be potted are moist at the roots.

Clay pots over $3\frac{1}{2}$ in diameter must be crocked unless soilless compost is being used. This involves placing a few pieces of broken flower pot concave side downwards over the hole in the base to prevent it from becoming blocked. Plastic pots contain many holes and so crocking is not necessary.

Choose a container which is large enough to hold the roots or rootball of the plant being potted with a little room to spare to allow for growth. Spread some compost in the base of the pot and sit the plant centrally on top of it. Scoop in more compost with your hand and firm it around the roots with your fingertips – lightly if it is a soilless compost, more firmly if it is John Innes. Don't leave any air pockets but don't overfill the pot. The roots of the plant should just be covered and the surface of the compost should be between 1 and 2.5 cm ($\frac{1}{2}$ and 1 in) below the pot rim to allow for watering. The larger the pot, the greater should be the gap.

If you pot a plant in a container which is too large it will develop roots at the expense of shoots and the compost may turn sour. It is far better to give a plant a container which it can fill relatively quickly, even if it does mean a little extra work for you.

Always water plants thoroughly after potting. Use a can fitted with a fine rose and apply water until it

Planting tomato plants directly into greenhouse border soil

starts to run out of the holes in the base of the pot. For a few days after the move keep the plants out of bright sunshine.

Planting

As much care must be taken with planting as with potting. In greenhouse borders make sure that the soil has been well cultivated and any manure or fertilizer added sufficiently in advance of planting. Soak the soil with a hosepipe a couple of days beforehand to make sure that it is moist. Put in any stakes or canes before you plant rather than after. Take out a hole which is larger than the rootball of the subject being planted, place the

plant into position and refirm the soil.

When planting in growing bags, first make the required holes and drainage slits, make sure that the compost is well distributed and plant up in the normal way. Water the plants in afterwards if manufacturers do not recommend soaking the compost before planting.

General cultivation

Plants which are growing well don't need to be coddled, but they do appreciate a little attention now and again. Here are some of the more important aspects of cultivation:

Feeding

Although it is seldom necessary until two months or so after potting (after six weeks if soilless composts are being used), feeding is essential if container-grown plants are to be kept in good health. During spring and summer all pot plants in active growth can be fed every ten days or so with a soluble fertilizer diluted in water. Border-grown plants will benefit from the added nutrition too.

Always apply liquid feed as directed by the manufacturer (never add more in the hope of giving plants an extra boost), and swap around now and again to give the plants a change. Feed when the soil in the pot or border is moist, then the roots are in a fit state to accept the nutrients and the fertilizer can go straight into action.

Topdressing

Large pot plants which do not need any more room, or which dislike root disturbance, can be given a boost by adding a little fresh compost to their existing container. Scrape away 5 to 8 cm (2 to 3 in) of the old soil at the top of the pot and replace it with a layer of John Innes potting compost No 3 or its soilless equivalent. This topdressing will provide extra nourishment and a home for new roots.

Plants growing in the greenhouse border can be topdressed more generously with well-rotted garden compost, farmyard manure, spent mushroom compost, hop manure and other bulky organic dressings. Peaches, grapes, cucumbers and

Three types of support: cane and twine tied in a figure of eight; trellis work for climbing plants and brushwood for bushy plants such as schizanthus.

melons will be particularly appreciative.

Apply topdressings in spring or early summer when the plants can really make use of them.

Supporting

Most plants are sturdy enough to support themselves but due to the demand for larger and larger flowers, many of the most showy greenhouse plants have relatively feeble stems which are not capable of holding their mammoth blooms upright.

Bamboo canes are the most obvious answer. These can be pushed into the compost 2.5 cm (1 in) or so away from single-stemmed plants and the stem fastened to the cane with a figure-of-eight tie. Use soft green twine, or raffia which has been soaked in water (this makes it easier to tie). Split green canes can be used to hold up more delicate plants.

Three or four canes pushed in around the rim of a pot can be linked with loops of twine to hold in any wayward stems of bushy pot plants, but a more natural support is achieved if one or two pieces of brushwood are pushed among the plant.

Ivies, philodendrons and other climbers can be trained on arches of wire or plastic trellises which can be pushed into the compost. Try to choose a design that is not too obtrusive.

Hyacinths have such weighty blooms that they often keel over. Prevent this by pushing a 23-cm (9-in) length of wire down through the stem and into the bulb. It may seem cruel but it does the job.

Plants being grown in the soil border and trained up the inside of the greenhouse can be tied in to wires stretched down the length of the house and held in place with metal 'vine eyes'. Space the wires at 23 cm (9 in) intervals from 60 cm (2 ft) above the floor to the ridge. They will screw quite easily into a wooden greenhouse but holes may have to be drilled and the eyes attached with bolts in aluminium models.

Growing bags have the distinction of being provided with a special plant support frame (at additional cost of course). This usually consists of a stout grid of plastic-covered wire, supported by two legs which the bag holds in position. It's an effective support system but rather an expensive one and you may

prefer to position one horizontal wire on the roof of your greenhouse, another on the floor, and run strong lengths of twine between the two. Tomatoes and other tall plants can be wound around the twine and effectively supported.

Labels

As your plant collection grows you will find it that much more difficult to remember what each plant is called – especially if you build up a collection of one type of plant. Labelling is the answer.

There are plenty of labels to choose from so you should find one that will please your eye and suit your needs. Simple plastic, wooden or anodised aluminium 'stick' labels are the most common and the most useful. Others are 'T'-shaped to

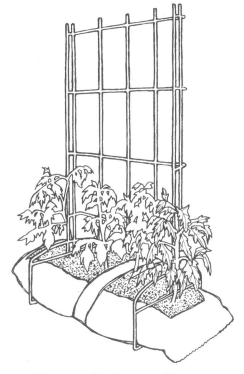

Special supports for plants reared in grow-bags

The heavy flower of the hyacinth is supported by wire pushed down through the centre of the stem.

make for easy reading and seem to be preferred by cactus and alpine growers.

Always write on labels with a soft pencil, indelible ink or a permanent felt-tip pen. Ballpoint ink disappears in sunlight. Plastic and aluminium labels can be scrubbed clean and used again, though the plastic ones become brittle as they age.

Where plants such as lettuce and radish are being grown in greenhouse borders, the type of label with a plastic window can be very useful. The seed packet is slipped inside, sealed in, and the information on cultivation is easily legible and safe from water.

Hygiene

However well you feed, water and care for your plants you will be putting their health at risk if the greenhouse is not kept clean and tidy.

Cleanliness

Keep the majority of pests, diseases and disorders at bay by following these guidelines:

1 Do not store dirty plant pots underneath the staging. If you must store pots here, wash them first and cover them with a sheet of polythene.

2 Keep the floor of the greenhouse free of spilled soil and other debris.

3 Remove faded flowers and leaves from all pot plants.

4 Remove and discard any plants showing signs of severe ill health.

5 Keep an eye open for pests and diseases and act quickly when they are seen (see pages 112 to 117).

It is a good idea to give your greenhouse a thorough clean out once a year. Remove the plants if possible, or store them under the staging and cover them with polythene. Scrub down the inside framework of the greenhouse with a diluted solution of Jeyes' Fluid and wash the glass inside and out with water containing detergent. A thin plastic or metal label can be used to push out any dirt lodged where the panes overlap. Wash gravel used on the staging by placing it in a sieve and running the hosepipe over it.

A winter hygiene routine: the dirt is removed from between panes of glass with an old plant label and the whole greenhouse is scrubbed down.

Weed control

Apart from being unsightly, weeds on the greenhouse floor can play host to pests and diseases which may also attack cultivated plants. Clear the ground by hand or with a hoe and water the soil with a residual weedkiller such as simazine. This forms a barrier in the soil which stops more weeds emerging. Apply the herbicide with a watering can fitted with dribble bar.

Do not be tempted to use sodium chlorate in the greenhouse. Apart from being a highly inflammable total weedkiller it will also move

Fumigating border soil by means of formalin.

sideways in the soil and may kill plants growing outside the greenhouse.

If you intend to stand plants on the floor underneath the staging do not use a herbicide. An 8-cm (3-in) layer of gravel spread over clean soil is a safer alternative which will prevent most weeds from emerging, and it is a good base on which to stand pot plants.

Algae

All greenhouse owners soon become familiar with the green slimy growth that appears on pots, paths, compost and capillary benches. Apart from being unsightly, algae can spread to such an extent that it hinders plant growth – particularly at the seedling stage.

On paths it can be removed by scrubbing with a stiff brush, and once clear the surface can be kept free of the green covering if a diluted solution of an algicide such as Algofen is watered on at intervals. Pots and boxes, capillary matting and compost surfaces can also be kept algae-free if they are treated with a weak solution.

Sterilizing borders

If you take over an old greenhouse with rather tired looking border soil, but feel that you don't want to go the the trouble of removing and replacing this with a fresh mixture, you can sterilize the ground with a chemical such as formalin. This is sold as a horticultural sterilant to kill soil-borne pests and diseases. The greenhouse must be emptied first (the fumes are poisonous to plants), and the soil should be forked over to allow the chemical to permeate through it.

Dilute the formalin to make a 2% solution as directed on the container (horticultural formalin comes with instructions on sterilization). The solution is then watered over the area to be sterilized until the soil is thoroughly moistened. Immediately after application a polythene sheet should be laid over the soil to keep in the fumes. Leave the sheet in position for two days, and do not attempt to grow plants in the soil until at least six weeks later.

If this operation sounds too complicated or time-consuming for you, do not despair: the simple alternative is to grow plants either on the ring culture system (see page 35) or in growing bags (see page 43).

The garden frame

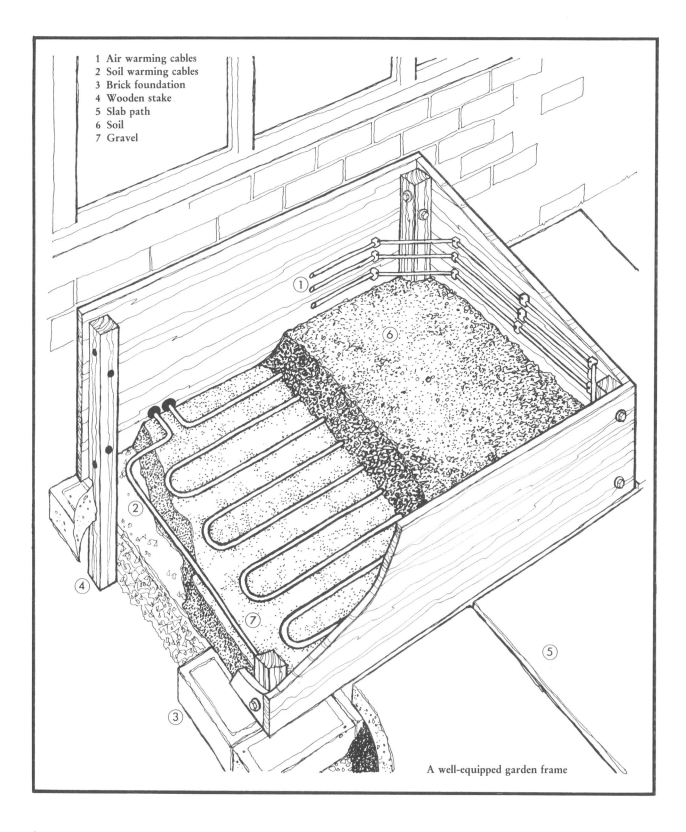

1 Air warming cables
2 Soil warming cables
3 Brick foundation
4 Wooden stake
5 Slab path
6 Soil
7 Gravel

A well-equipped garden frame

Install a frame in your garden and you will soon enjoy its benefits. For raising plants, hardening off those grown in the greenhouse, forcing fruit and vegetables and overwintering plants of a tender disposition this simple structure is invaluable.

Types

There are many different designs to choose from, but one of the best is the single-span type which you can either buy or make at home. Sheet steel, aluminium or timber may form the sides of proprietary models; home-made versions can be constructed from whatever wood happens to be available. Timber insulates far better than steel or aluminium and is therefore preferable, but it should de treated with preservative to prolong its life.

The lid or 'light' of the frame may be made from glass or plastic. The first lasts longer, admits more light and keeps in more heat. However, if children are around a rigid plastic or polythene lid will be safer.

Make sure that the frame is large enough and deep enough to accommodate the plants you want to grow.

Siting

Position a single-span frame so that it faces south and receives as much sun as possible. Sited near to the greenhouse or actually against the greenhouse wall it will be much more convenient when plants are moved from one structure to the other – particularly when large batches of vegetable and flower seedlings are to be 'hardened off' (gradually accustomed to lower temperatures before being planted out).

A double span frame can face any direction provided it is in a position that admits plenty of light.

Foundations

Small home-made or shop-bought frames can be erected without foundations, provided that they are staked firmly to the ground with stout wooden posts. The portability of these small models is one of their advantages. Larger frames which are to be positioned permanently in one spot should be equipped with foundations in the same way as greenhouses (see page 22) so that the lights fit well and do not buckle. If precast foundations are offered by the manufacturer, make use of them.

Treatment

Just like cedar or softwood greenhouses, timber frames should be treated with preservative, or painted, every two or three years. Never use creosote on frames for it gives off toxic fumes which will damage plants. Aluminium frames will get by if their hinges and catches are oiled now and again – something which you should also take care of on timber frames.

Access

Make sure you can get to your frame even in wet weather. A concrete slab path laid around it will keep your feet dry and encourage you to look at the plants regularly. Gravel is an easy-to-lay alternative.

Base material

If your aim is to grow early vegetables in the frame the soil should be retained (if it is at all reasonable) and enriched with compost or manure and fertilizer in the same way as the greenhouse border (see page 35). Replace the soil to a depth of 23 cm (9 in) if it is really poor. Apply fertilizer and manure once a year and give the soil a good flood with the hosepipe when each crop has been removed. This will clear it of impurities and provide an adequate supply of moisture for the plants that follow.

When the frame is to be used to house container-grown pot plants, spread a layer of shingle or weathered ashes in the base. This will ensure good drainage and prevent worms from working their way into pots and boxes. (Worms are essential in the soil but interfere with drainage in containers.)

Heating

Attach a frame directly to your greenhouse and you may be able to make use of the heating system. Hot water pipes can be led through the back of the frame, or warming cables laid beneath the soil and around the sides. These cables form perhaps the most convenient and economical means of heating, especially if they are connected to a thermostat. Lay them 8 to 10 cm (3 to 4 in) deep if plants are being grown in the soil, and 2.5 to 5 cm (1 to 2 in) apart on the sides of the frame. Manufacturers will advise on how much cable is needed to heat a frame of a given area.

Small paraffin heaters may be used to warm a frame, but ventilation must be given at all times and a free circulation of air allowed round the burner. Check that the heater you buy is the right size for your frame and, for safety's sake, only use a model specifically designed for horticultural use.

Ventilation

In warm spells, and all through the summer, frame lights can simply be removed altogether, stacked safely in a corner and tied down so that they will not be blown over by wind.

The garden frame

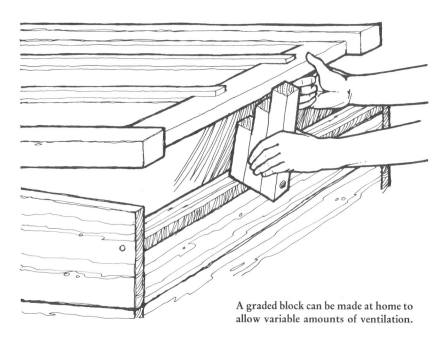

A graded block can be made at home to allow variable amounts of ventilation.

time at all to water with a watering can or hosepipe; larger frames can be fitted with a semi-automatic watering system to make life easier.

Alkathene piping fitted with small-bore 'spaghetti' tubes can be laid right through the frame and a tube taken to each plant; or the pipe may be equipped with atomizers every 1.5 m (5 ft) and suspended over the plants so that a coarse spray is distributed over them. A simpler alternative is to lay a perforated hose through the frame; when the water is turned on small jets are sent out at all angles. These methods of watering have the disadvantage that all the plants are watered at once, regardless of whether they are wet or dry.

Rather better is the capillary watering system which can be

To allow just a little ventilation the lights may be either slid down, if they are on runners, or wedged open to the required extent with a 'stepped' block of wood if they are hinged. Some proprietary frames have hinged lights fitted with adjustable casement stays; these are fine provided that the lights are firmly held.

Whenever your frame is completely closed, take the precaution of laying heavy lengths of timber across the lights so that they are not lifted by wind. Cleats can be attached to the ends and runners of a wooden frame and strong rope run between them to hold the lights in position.

Insulation

Help to keep your frame warm in winter by lining the lights with polythene. At night old sacks or carpet can be thrown over the top and weighed down with bricks, but make sure that you remove this

covering during the day to admit light.

To insulate the walls you can make mattresses of straw and chicken wire and position them right round the frame.

Shading

Being smaller than the average greenhouse, a garden frame will heat up much more quickly in bright spells of sunshine, so it is important to provide some sort of shading material from April onwards. Whitewash, shading compound, muslin, lath or bamboo blinds can all be used, as can green closeweave plastic netting. The netting, muslin and blinds have the advantage of being easily removed if the sun goes in. (See also greenhouse shading on pages 32 and 33).

Watering

Pot plants in small frames take no

modified for use in the garden frame. Capillary matting is expensive in very large quantities so it may be more convenient to use sand. Level and firm the soil in the frame, lay a sheet of heavy gauge polythene over it and spread a 5-cm (2-in) layer of coarse river sand over this. Level and tamp down the sand before putting the pot plants in position.

A trickle irrigation line is then snaked between the plants. Make sure that it is evenly distributed so that the entire sand area is moistened when the water is turned on, and remember to use plastic pots rather than clay ones which will have to be fitted with a wick. Any algae that appears on the sand can be controlled by watering with Algofen (see page 59).

Plants grown directly in the soil can be watered automatically using

Straw bales and canvas used to give frost protection

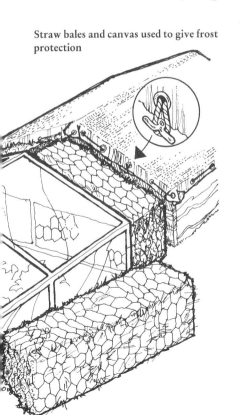

A frame used as a plunge bed to start off bulbs

the perforated hose or atomizer systems.

Plunge bed

You might think that a garden frame would be redundant through the summer. This is far from true. Filled with a 30-cm (12-in) layer of moist peat or sand it makes an ideal home for alpines and other pot plants which can be plunged to their pot rims in the cool, moist medium. Even quite tender plants will enjoy a summer in the open and their compost will dry out more slowly in the plunge bed.

While these plants are outside you have the opportunity to use the valuable space they vacated in the greenhouse to grow melons, cucumbers, peppers, aubergines and tomatoes.

When the pot plants are returned to the greenhouse at the end of the summer the peat or sand can be left in the frame and used to cover newly potted spring-flowering bulbs. Narcissi in particular enjoy a period of at least eight weeks in a cool, dark place so that they can establish a good root system. Cover them entirely with the medium and place the lights on the frame to keep out rain. Apply no heat but allow a little ventilation at all times. After two months dig up the bulbs and grow them on in a cool greenhouse.

Flowering pot plants

A few packets of seeds or a handful of cuttings are all you need to ensure that there are flowers in your greenhouse every single day of the year. Even the most dedicated tomato and cucumber grower can afford space for half-a-dozen pot plants. These can be raised and grown on in the greenhouse and moved indoors to brighten your rooms when their flowers start to open. A conservatory filled with flowering pot plants provides you with an indoor garden full of blooms which you can enjoy whatever the weather.

Don't think that you need a lot of heat to keep up this year-round display; many of the plants in this section will be happy if they are kept just frost-free at around 7°C (45°F) through the winter. If you want flowers that demand no heat at all there is a selection on the pages devoted to climbers and bulbs.

The plants described here fall into the following groups: annuals, which grow, flower and die within one year; biennials which take two years, and perennials which will survive indefinitely. Hardy varieties can stay outdoors all their lives if necessary; half-hardy types need to be raised in the greenhouse but may be put outside in the summer; tender types need the shelter of the greenhouse at all times. You may choose to grow all three types under glass for part or all of the year to provide continuous colour.

Apart from the varieties mentioned in detail in the pages that follow, remember that many hardy and half-hardy annual bedding plants can also be grown in pots to provide colour in your greenhouse. If sown in spring they will bloom in summer; sown in August they can be kept frost free through the winter and grown on to give a colourful show the following spring. Clarkia, godetia, salpiglossis, lavatera, mignonette, calendula, nicotiana, nemesia and larkspur will all respond well to this treatment.

Abbreviations:
HA – Hardy annual
HHA – Half-hardy annual
HP – Hardy perennial
HHP – Half-hardy perennial
TA – Tender annual
TB – Tender biennial
TP – Tender perennial
HB – Hardy biennial
HHB – Half-hardy biennial
JIP – John Innes Potting Compost

A colourful display of flowering pot plants including busy lizzie, cineraria, slipper flower and primula.

African violet

Saintpaulia ionantha varieties TP

These popular house and greenhouse plants have compact rosettes of light green, dark green, and in some cases variegated leaves, and clusters of purple, blue, magenta, pink or white flowers. The blooms may be single or double, plain or frilled. If a little winter warmth can be given they will flower all the year round.

How to start
Seeds may be sown on the surface of the seed compost in pots or trays from February to March. Do not cover with compost. Leaf cuttings can be rooted in summer (see page 53). Multi-crowned plants can be divided in summer.
Sowing temperature 18 to 20°C (65 to 70°F)
Rooting temperature 18°C (65°F)
Growing-on temperature 10°C (50°F) winter minimum; rather more if you want flowers all the year round.

How to grow
Prick out the seedlings (as soon as they are large enough to handle) into trays of a soilless, peat-based potting compost; personally, I find they grow better in this than in JIP compost. When the young plants begin to touch one another, pot them up in 8-cm (3-in) pots of the same mixture. Leaf cuttings may produce several plantlets and these should be separated and potted up individually, also in 8-cm (3-in) pots. African violets like warm, humid conditions, so grow them at the end of the greenhouse nearest the heater, or else in a large-windowed propagating frame where they will thrive in a temperature of 18 to 20°C (65 to 70°F). Shade them from strong sunshine and water them carefully when they are dry, taking care not to splash the leaves. Water from the base if the watering can cannot penetrate the rosette. Remove flowers and leaves as they fade to prevent rot setting in. Feed every two weeks. Plants may be potted on into 10-cm (4-in) half-pots if required. Bring indoors in winter

Cape primrose Constant Nymph

if the greenhouse temperature will be too low.

Good varieties
Many named varieties (most of them American) can be obtained from nurserymen and propagated by leaf cuttings. Seedsmen offer a very limited range – usually one pink and one blue strain, of which the Fairytale varieties are good examples.

Busy Lizzie

Impatiens species and varieties TP

Seldom out of flower if kept warm throughout the winter, busy lizzies will produce myriads of scarlet, orange, pink or white blooms on top of fleshy stems clothed in bright green, purple or variegated leaves.

How to start
Sow the seeds in pots or trays of seed compost from March to June, covering them lightly. Cuttings can be rooted in pots, jars of water or a propagating frame through the summer. This is the best way to increase the coloured-foliage varieties.
Sowing temperature 18 to 20°C (65 to 70°F)
Rooting temperature 18°C (65°F)
Growing-on temperature 7°C (45°F) minimum; 10 to 13°C (50 to 55°F) is better.

How to grow
Pot up seedlings and rooted cuttings individually in 8-cm (3-in) pots of JIP 1 or a soilless equivalent. Pot on into 10- or 12-cm (4- or 5-in) pots as the plants grow. Pinch out the shoot tips to encourage bushiness. Apply copious amounts of water in summer, but keep the compost on the dry side in winter. Shade from bright sunshine but grow in good light. Keep an eye open for red spider mite and greenfly, spraying when necessary. Feed every week from June to September.

Good varieties
Seedsmen offer many mixed and single-coloured varieties which range in height from 23 to 60 cm (9 to 24 in). Harlequin, 30 cm (1 ft), is

one variety worth trying; it produces red, orange or pink flowers splashed with white. Buy the coloured-foliage varieties from a garden centre or nursery and propagate from cuttings.

Cape Primrose

Streptocarpus hybrids TP

Dainty or blowsy trumpet flowers of rich blue, magenta, pink or white nod gracefully over long, green, downy leaves on a plant that deserves to be more widely grown.

How to start
Sow the fine seeds on the surface of seed compost in pots or trays from January to March (the earlier the better – if you can afford the heat). Do not cover them with compost. Leaf cuttings can be taken in summer and rooted in a propagating frame (see page 53). Older plants can be divided in spring.
Sowing temperature 18°C (65°F)
Rooting temperature 18°C (65°F)
Growing-on temperature 7°C (45°F) winter minimum; 10 to 13°C (50 to 55°F) if you want to keep them flowering in autumn.

How to grow
Pot up the seedlings into 8-cm (3-in) pots of soilless compost as soon as they are large enough to handle. Rooted leaf cuttings can be similarly potted when they have produced shoots. Stand the plants in a warm place until they become established. Pot on into 10-cm (4-in) pots when necessary. Water well when dry and feed fortnightly as soon as flower buds form. January-sown plants should start to bloom in August. Shade from bright sunshine and ventilate well through summer. Damp down twice daily to keep the atmosphere humid. When the flowers fade, pinch them off and keep the compost on the dry side through winter. Repot these plants when growth starts again the following spring.

Good varieties

Constant Nymph, 23 to 30 cm (9 to 12 in), is a great favourite. The flowers are dainty and a beautiful shade of blue with darker markings in the throat. This variety must be propagated by leaf cuttings; seed is not available. Several mixed strains produce excellent plants with showy, strongly coloured blooms. The Triumph Mixture is a good one to try.

Carnation

Dianthus species HHP

Perpetual-flowering carnations are worth growing even in small numbers because they can be brought into flower, as their name implies, all the year round. These are the carnations you buy in the florists – well-shaped blooms of red, yellow, pink and white on long stems.

How to start

Buy rooted cuttings of named varieties from a specialist nursery between January and March. Pot these up in 8-cm (3-in) pots of JIP 1. In subsequent years plants may be raised from cuttings of sideshoots, 10 cm (4 in) long, removed from halfway up the stems at any time between December and February.
Rooting temperature 16°C (60°F)

Carnation Dusty Sim

Growing-on temperature 4 to 7°C (40 to 45°F) minimum. Keep cool at all times.

How to grow

Pot on into 12-cm (5-in) pots of JIP 2 as the plants grow, and stand them outdoors on hard ground or in a plunge bed through the summer. Move them on to 20-cm (8-in) pots when necessary. Return the plants to the greenhouse in September. They will eventually grow well over 1 m (3 ft) tall, so stand them on the floor to allow plenty of headroom. Pinch out the shoot tip of each plant as soon as eight or ten pairs of leaves have been formed; pinch out each sideshoot after seven or eight pairs have developed. Try to 'stop' the plants (pinch out the shoot tips) at different times to encourage successional flowering. Avoid stopping after the end of June if you want winter flowers. As the flower stems grow, canes can be pushed into the pot and the stems held in with loops of soft twine. Special carnation supports are also available. Water freely in summer, more sparingly in winter and feed fortnightly with tomato fertilizer when the plants have become established in their final pots. Remove all but the large central bud on each stem. Shade in summer and ventilate well at all times. Cut the blooms with long stems just before they are fully open, and put them into water at once. Discard the plants after two years and replace with newly rooted cuttings.

Good varieties

Dusty Sim, pink; Arthur Sim, white, striped red; Tangerine Sim, orange; White Sim; William Sim, red; Clear Yellow Sim.

Chrysanthemum

HHP

Autumn wouldn't be the same without chrysanthemums, and even though their flowers can be bought in the shops all the year round, the plants are usually grown by the home gardener to flower in their natural season. Early-flowering

chrysanthemums are grown outdoors; October- and late-flowering varieties are planted in pots for greenhouse flowering.

How to start

To be sure of obtaining healthy plants that are true to name, buy rooted cuttings of named varieties from a specialist grower in March or April. In subsequent years the older plants can be cut down to pot level after flowering, knocked out of their pots, the compost shaken from the roots, and the 'stools', as they are called, boxed up in trays of JIP 1.

Chrysanthemum **Jeancot Yellow Supreme**

Placed in a well-lit spot in a cool greenhouse the stools will produce small, sturdy shoots which are removed as cuttings in January or February when they are 5 to 8 cm (2 to 3 in) high. Prepare the cuttings and dib them into pots or a propagator. Discard the stools.
Rooting temperature 13 to 16°C (55 to 60°F)
Growing-on temperature 10°C (50°F) minimum. Keep cool at all times.

How to grow

Pot up the young plants in 8-cm (3-in) pots of JIP 1. Stand in good light and ventilate well during the day. While the plants are still small they can be grown in a garden frame which is protected from frost. Pot on the plants as they grow; first into 12-cm (5-in) pots of JIP 2, and then into 20-cm (8-in) pots of JIP 3. If you wish, two plants from the 8-cm (3-in) pots may be planted direct into a 25-cm (10-in) pot of JIP 3.

Pinch out the shoot tip of each plant when it is 20 cm (8 in) tall. Once the plants are in their final pots they should be provided with a stout 1.25-m (4-ft) cane. Pinch out the tips of the side shoots when they reach a length of 20 cm (8 in). Allow only three stems per plant if you want good-sized blooms, more if small blooms are preferred. Loop the stems to the cane with soft twine as they grow. Stand the plants outdoors on a concrete or gravel surface from late May onwards when danger of frost is past. Make sure they are sheltered from strong winds; tie the canes to a wire strained between two posts to hold the plants steady. Water freely throughout the summer and feed every week with liquid fertilizer. Several flower buds will appear on each stem. If large blooms are to be produced remove all but the central bud; if sprays are required remove the central bud only and leave the rest. Move the plants to the shelter of the greenhouse in late September, standing them on the floor to allow maximum headroom. Keep the atmosphere dry and airy but water the plants well when they are dry. Continue to tie in the stems loosely as they extend. Remove all minor sideshoots and dead leaves. Keep an eye open for mildew and leaf miner, spraying the plants (but not the flowers) if necessary.

Good varieties
Specialist nurserymen will provide catalogues containing vast numbers of excellent varieties.

Cineraria

Senecio cruentus HHP treated as HHA

Mounds of green maple-shaped leaves topped with colourful bunches of daisy-like flowers make the cineraria a popular pot plant. It flowers in winter and spring.

How to start
Sow seeds in trays or pots of compost from April to June and cover lightly.
Sowing temperature 10 to 16°C (50 to 60°F)

Cineraria hybrid

Growing-on temperature 7°C (45°F) minimum. Keep cool at all times.

How to grow
Prick out the seedlings into trays of JIP 1 or a soilless equivalent as soon as they are large enough to handle. Pot up into 10-cm (4-in) pots of JIP 2 or a soilless equivalent before the plants become too overcrowded. Cinerarias can spend the summer in the garden frame or a plunge bed. Shade them from bright sunshine and water carefully; they will not tolerate being kept too wet. Spray to control greenfly and leaf miner if necessary, and feed fortnightly from August onwards. Move the plants back into the greenhouse in late September and keep them cool but frost free. Discard after flowering.

Good varieties
Many mixtures are sold. These vary in height from 20 to 75 cm (8 to 30 in) and have flowers of white, red, magenta, blue, purple and pink.

Cyclamen

Cyclamen persicum hybrids TP

These handsome but rather tricky winter-flowering plants have rounded domes of attractively marbled leaves, over which are held reflexed pink, white, magenta, salmon or red flowers.

How to start
Sow seeds thinly in pots or trays of seed compost in August. Cover lightly.

Sowing temperature 16 to 18°C (60 to 65°F)
Growing-on temperature 10 to 13°C (50 to 55°F). Keep cool at all times.

How to grow
Prick out the seedlings into trays of JIP 1 as soon as they are large enough to handle. Pot up into 8-cm (3-in) pots of JIP 2 in spring, and finally into 12-cm (5-in) pots during the following summer. Make sure that the corm (the bulb-like growth at the base of the leaves) sits on the surface of the compost. Stand the plants in a garden frame or plunge bed through the summer, returning them to the greenhouse in late September. Remove dead leaves and spray if greenfly are a problem. Remove any flowers that appear before November. Water only when dry and avoid splashing the leaves. Ventilate whenever possible.

***Cyclamen persicum* hybrid**

Feed fortnightly through the summer and when the plants are in flower. Remove faded blooms. Plants will flower at Christmas, sixteen months after being sown. After flowering the corms may be rested and started into growth again the following year. Place the pots on their sides underneath the greenhouse staging and allow the compost to dry off. The following July or August, lift the plants on to the staging, water them gently and when they start to grow again repot them in JIP 2. Give them the same growing conditions as seedlings and they will flower in the first winter after being started.

Good varieties
There are many good mixed varieties – try to find those such as Decora, 30 cm (12 in) which have well-marked leaves, or the ruffled types which have fimbriated (fringed) flowers.

Fuchsia

HHP

The gracefully arching stems of the fuchsia show off to perfection the single or double pendant flowers of white, pink, carmine, red and purple. These can be grown to advantage in hanging baskets as well as pots.

How to start
Take cuttings of soft shoot tips from April to August and root in pots or a propagating frame.
Rooting temperature 16 to 18°C (60 to 65°F)
Growing-on temperature 7°C (45°F) minimum; 10°C (50°F) if the plants are to be kept active.

How to grow
Pot up the rooted cuttings in 8-cm (3-in) pots of JIP 1. Either pinch to encourage bushiness, or remove sideshoots to produce one long stem, the tip of which can be pinched out at 1 m (3 ft) to form a standard. A single stem should be supported with a stout cane. Pot on the plants as necessary until they are in 12- or 15-cm (5- or 6-in) pots of JIP 2. During the summer the plants can be moved to the garden frame or plunge bed, but bring them back into the greenhouse in late September. Feed fortnightly when the plants are established in their final pots. Shade from strong sunshine. The fuchsias will flower in summer twelve months after being propagated. Remove any small flushes of flower buds which appear

before this time, unless you want blooms as soon as possible. Spray if whitefly or red spider mite are a problem. Mature plants can be rested in the winter after flowering. Keep them free from frost and on the dry side. Cut the old shoots hard back in spring and repot the plants in JIP 2, removing some of the old compost. Spray overhead with tepid water to bring into growth.

Good varieties
Ballet Girl, red sepals, white petals; Checkerboard, white sepals turning pink, rich red petals; Golden Treasure, yellow and green variegated leaves, rosy pink sepals, purple petals; Marinka, red sepals, purple petals; Swingtime, red sepals, double white petals. There are many more excellent varieties available from specialist nurserymen as rooted cuttings or pot-grown plants.

Gloxinia

Sinningia speciosa hybrids TP

Large, boldly-coloured, velvety trumpets of red, purple, pink and white, often contrastingly spotted or bordered, are held above large, downy leaves. Mid- to late summer flowering.

How to start
Sow the dust-fine seeds on the surface of pots or trays of seed compost from January to March. Do not cover with compost.
Sowing temperature 16 to 18°C (60 to 65°F)
Growing-on temperature 16°C (60°F)

How to grow
Prick out into trays of JIP 1 or a soilless equivalent, and as soon as the plants are touching one another transplant them individually into 8-cm (3-in) pots of the same mixture. Later they can be moved into 10- or 12-cm (4- or 5-in) pots of JIP 2 or its equivalent. Shade the plants from strong sunshine in summer and water them well when they are dry. Feed fortnightly through the summer. When the flowers fall in autumn, allow the plants to dry off on their sides under the greenhouse

staging. When they have died down, knock them from their pots and store the tubers in dry peat. They can be grown again the following spring. In March or April these tubers should be bedded into the surface of moist peat contained in seed trays. Sprayed overhead and gently watered they will soon start to grow and can be potted up in 12-cm (5-in) pots (with the tuber just covered) and grown on as for seedlings. Plants may also be increased by leaf cuttings in the same way as *Begonia rex* (see page 53), or the stalk of the leaf may be pushed into cutting compost and allowed to root.

Good varieties
Many mixed and single-coloured varieties are available and these range in height from 23 to 30 cm (9 to 12 in).

Ornamental pepper

Capsicum annuum HHA

These upright, bushy plants are a welcome sight in winter when their rounded or long, pointed berries turn from green to shades of yellow, orange, purple and bright red.

How to start
Sow the seeds in pots or trays of seed compost from February to April, covering them lightly.
Sowing temperature 18 to 20°C (65 to 70°F)
Growing-on temperature 7°C (45°F) winter minimum.

How to grow
Prick out the seedlings individually into 8-cm (3-in) pots of JIP 1 or a soilless equivalent. Water freely through summer and stand outdoors in a garden frame or plunge bed (or else keep in a cool greenhouse). Pot on when necessary into 10-cm (4-in) pots. Pinch out the shoot tips to encourage bushiness. When the white flowers appear, spray the plants with water to encourage fruit setting. Water once a month with Epsom salts diluted in water at the rate of one dessertspoonful to a

Pelargoniums for the enthusiast

gallon. Feed fortnightly from flowering onwards. Bring back into the greenhouse in mid-September to protect from frost.

Good varieties
Chamaeleon, 23 cm (9 in), cream, orange and red berries, green leaves; Fips, 15 to 23 cm (6 to 9 in), cream orange and red berries, green leaves; Variegated Flash, 25 cm (10 in), green, purple and black berries, purple green and white variegated leaves.

Pelargonium

Zonal types HHP

Although commonly known as the 'geranium' it is not listed here under its common name because this properly applies to many of the hardy perennial garden species. Bright double or single flowers of scarlet, crimson, magenta, orange, pink or white, many of them contrastingly marked, are carried in abundance all summer long and sometimes in winter too. There are many varieties with brightly coloured leaves, some of them showing the characteristic dark zoning that resulted in the name 'zonal pelargoniums'.

How to start
Individual named varieties must be grown from cuttings rooted in pots or a propagating frame in spring or summer. F_1 hybrid strains can be grown from seeds which should be space sown in pots of seed compost between January and March.
Sowing temperature 18°C (65°F)
Rooting temperature 16 to 18°C (60 to 65°F)
Growing-on temperature 4 to 7°C (40 to 45°F) winter minimum.

How to grow
Pot up seedlings and rooted cuttings in 8-cm (3-in) pots of JIP 1 as soon as they are large enough to handle or well rooted. Keep the plants in a well-lit part of the greenhouse and water them well when dry. Cuttings

taken in spring can be potted on into 10-cm (4-in) pots of JIP 1 in summer. Summer-rooted cuttings can stay in their 8-cm (3-in) pots until the following spring. Pinch out the shoot tip of each plant when it is 8 cm (3 in) high, and pinch subsequent shoots in the same way to encourage bushiness. Feed fortnightly from May to September. Ventilate well in summer, or stand the plants outdoors from June to September. Bring them in before the frosts strike. During winter the plants should be kept on the dry side. Single varieties will flower in winter if their flower buds are removed through the summer and only allowed to develop in autumn. Double varieties are more shy but some of them will bloom in winter. Old plants can be grown on until they become unsightly, then they are best discarded and their shoots used as cuttings.

Good varieties
Mrs Henry Cox, rich pink blooms, red, brown, green and cream leaves; Verona, pink blooms, acid-yellow leaves; Highfields Attracta, double pink and white blooms in large trusses, green leaves; Frank Headley, pink blooms, green leaves edged with white; Apple Blossom Rosebud, tight white double blooms edged with deep pink, green leaves; Maréchal McMahon, scarlet blooms, yellow-green leaves with maroon zone; Paul Crampel, scarlet blooms, green leaves with dark brown zone.
From seed: Sprinter is one of the best mixtures. All these varieties will grow to between 23 and 45 cm (9 and 18 in) high.

Poor man's orchid

Schizanthus hybrids HHA

The butterfly flower, or poor man's orchid, as it is commonly known, is one of the most delicate and delightful greenhouse plants. In spring or summer, depending on the time of sowing, its ferny green foliage is smothered with intricately tinted blooms of pink, white, purple and magenta.

Poor man's orchid (Schizanthus)

How to start
Sow the seeds in pots or trays of seed compost in August to produce flowering plants for the following spring. Sow in March or April for summer flowers.
Sowing temperature 16 to 18°C (60 to 65°F)
Growing-on temperature 7°C (45°F) minimum. Keep cool at all times.

How to grow
Pot up the seedlings individually in 8-cm (3-in) pots of JIP 1 or a soilless equivalent as soon as they are large enough to handle. Large varieties should later be potted on into 12-cm (5-in) pots of JIP 2 when they have filled the first container, or three may be planted in an 18- or 20-cm (7- or 8-in) pot. The dwarf varieties will be happy left in 8-cm (3-in) pots if they are fed well when blooms form. With the large varieties pinch out the shoot tip of each plant when it is 8 cm (3 in) high and pinch the sideshoots that follow, so producing a bushy plant. Ventilate well in warm weather and water when dry. As the plants grow push in pieces of twiggy brushwood to support the stems of 30-cm (1-ft) high varieties. Use canes and soft twine for the tall varieties. Feed fortnightly when the flowers start to form. Keep an eye open for red spider mite and greenfly. Discard the plants when they finish flowering.

Good varieties
Hit Parade, 30 cm (12 in), mixed (this also grows well as a trailer if left unstaked); Star Parade, 15 cm

(6 in), mixed; Giant Pansy Flowered, 1 m (3 ft), mixed.

Primulas

Primula obconica TP and *Primula malacoides* TA

Two excellent free-flowering plants for a cool greenhouse. Obconica, the perennial, produces large mounds of green leaves topped with magenta, pink, blue or white primrose flowers. It blooms in winter and spring, and at intervals through the rest of the year. Malacoides, the annual, has smaller rosettes of foliage and delicate stalks which carry tiers of smaller blooms in a similar range of colours also in winter and spring.

How to start
Sow the seeds of both species on the surface of seed compost in pots or trays; obconica in March or April; malacoides in May or June. Do not cover the seeds with compost.
Sowing temperature 16°C (60°F)
Growing-on temperature 7°C (45°F) winter minimum. Keep cool at all times.

Primula obconica

How to grow
Prick out the seedlings into trays of JIP 1 or a soilless equivalent as soon as they are large enough to handle. When the leaves begin to touch in the trays, pot up the young plants into 10-cm (4-in) pots of JIP 2 or its equivalent. Malacoides will be happy left in this size container; obconica

Primula malacoides mixed

will need to be moved on later into 12-cm (5-in) pots. Water the plants well through the summer and shade them from strong sunshine. From June to September they can be stood in a garden frame or plunge bed. Water well when dry. Remove any flowers that form in late summer or autumn to save the plants' energy for the later more impressive flush. Feed fortnightly from July onwards. Bring the plants into the greenhouse in September but ventilate well whenever possible. Keep water off the leaves during autumn and winter; the plants should be watered from below. Discard malacoides after flowering; obconica may be grown on until the plants become very leafy and reluctant to flower.

Good varieties
Seedsmen offer many individually coloured or mixed strains, most of which are vigorous and well coloured.
NB The leaves of *Primula obconica* can sometimes irritate the skin. If you find that the plant brings you out in a rash, discard it and grow *Primula malacoides*.

Slipper flower

Calceolaria hybrids HHB

Spectacular red, yellow, orange or white pouch-like blooms, often contrastingly spotted, are massed together over coarse green leaves in spring. The plants are rounded

and bushy or taller with more open growth.

How to start
Sow the dust-fine seeds on the surface of seed compost in pots or trays from May to July. Do not cover with compost.
Sowing temperature 16 to 18°C (60 to 65°F)
Growing-on temperature 7°C (45°F) winter minimum. Keep cool at all times.

How to grow
Prick out the seedlings into boxes of JIP 1 or a soilless compost as soon as they are large enough to handle. During the summer the plants can be kept in a shady garden frame. Pot up into 8-cm (3-in) pots of JIP 2 or a soilless equivalent when the plants are 8 cm (3 in) high. Transfer to 12-cm (5-in) pots of the same mixture in late summer. Overwinter in a cool greenhouse taking care not to overwater. Feed once a week when flower buds appear in spring. Keep an eye open for greenfly and spray when necessary, avoiding the flowers.

Good varieties
Multiflora Mixed, 30 cm (12 in), mixed colours; Jewel Cluster, 30 cm (12 in), mixed colours, very early flowering (will bloom at Christmas from a July sowing). Monarch strain 30 cm (12 in) high with large brightly coloured flowers.

Slipper flower (calceolaria hybrids)

Flowering bulbs

Compared with many plants bulbs are very easy to grow. They contain flower, leaf and root embryos and almost all you have to do is add water and stand back! All but one of the plants listed on the next two pages are true bulbs; that is, they consist of closely packed scales, which are really leaf bases, crowded together on a very condensed stem known as the base plate. The odd man out is the freesia – this grows from a corm, which is a short, thickened stem.

Equipped, as they are, with these storage organs, what do bulbs need to produce good flowers? Moisture, and not much more, is the answer. The treatment the bulbs were given in the previous season will be reflected in the way they grow – in other words, if you buy from a reputable supplier all you need to do is provide a moisture-retentive medium to grow the bulbs in, a supply of water, and a little food in the case of freesias and hippeastrums. For tulips, narcissi and hyacinths, bulb fibre can be used in bowls with no drainage holes provided that you water carefully. The fibre should contain charcoal to prevent sourness. In pots, JIP compost with sand added will give better results.

If you possess an unheated greenhouse you can rely on all three of these last-named bulbs to produce a winter and spring display with no bother at all. Freesias and hippeastrums can be rested and grown in pots again the following year, the rest are best planted in the garden, but with all the bulbs you will enjoy bright blooms for several seasons.

Apart from the bulbs mentioned here in detail, crocuses, snowdrops, grape hyacinths, dwarf irises, chionodoxas and scillas are among those that can be grown to produce a colourful winter and spring show in an unheated greenhouse.

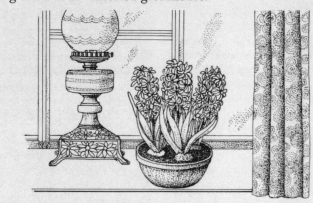

Narcissi and hyacinths provide a good
source of colour for a springtime display.

Freesia

The scent of home-grown freesias in winter is one of the greenhouse gardener's great joys. The plants are easy to grow and will produce many arching stems of yellow, orange, magenta, lavender and white blooms among sheaves of grassy leaves.

How to plant

Half-a-dozen corms will fit in a 12-cm (5-in) pot and they should be covered with 2.5 cm (1 in) of compost. Use JIP 1 and water the corms in after planting.
When to plant August and September.

How to grow

Stand the planted pots in a cool and shady garden frame until growth starts, then move them into a well-ventilated greenhouse (minimum temperature 7°C, (45°F)) and water the plants when they are dry. Support the plants as they grow with canes pushed in around the edge of the pot and linked with soft twine, or else with small pieces of brushwood pushed into the compost. As soon as flower buds are seen feed the plants fortnightly.

Maintain a cool, dry atmosphere. Stems may be cut and brought indoors just before the blooms open. When the flowers on the plants fade, ease off watering but keep the compost just moist until the foliage starts to die down. Then place the pots on their sides underneath the greenhouse staging and let them dry out completely. During the summer the corms can be salvaged from the compost and the largest ones potted up the following August for another display.

Good varieties

Buttercup, deep yellow; Pink Giant, pink; Red Chief, crimson; White Swan, white; Royal Present, lavender and yellow; Sapphire, lavender. Some varieties are much more strongly scented than others.

Hippeastrum

Ugly or spectacular; opinion seems to be divided on the merits of the stately hippeastrum (still sometimes known as amaryllis). Whether you like or loathe the plant it's one that can't be ignored – it produces massive pink, white or red flowers on 60-cm (2-ft) stems in winter or spring.

Hippeastrum hybrid

How to plant

One bulb to a 15-cm (6-in) pot of JIP 2. Leave half the bulb protruding from the compost.
When to plant January to March (ordinary); October to November (prepared).

How to grow

Keep in a greenhouse with a minimum temperature of 10°C (50°F). 'Prepared' bulbs can be brought into flower for Christmas if kept in a temperature of 20°C (70°F) from planting. Water the bulbs very carefully at first, taking care not to give too much. As the flower spike extends push a cane into the compost and fasten the two loosely together. The root system of the bulb does not fully develop until the leaves grow. When the flowers fade and the leaves do start to grow, water the plants well when they are dry and feed fortnightly. In autumn and winter the bulbs can be rested and dried off under the staging, or they can be kept ticking over in their pots, with the compost on the dry side, if a minimum temperature of 7°C (45°F) can be maintained. If you do this scrape away some of the old compost and topdress the plants in spring.

Good varieties

Hippeastrums are usually sold in colours rather than named varieties; look out for those that are contrastingly striped. The hybrid forms are the kinds most usually grown and carry their large trumpet-shaped flowers in clusters.

Freesia hybrid

Hyacinth

Hyacinths are unsurpassed for powerful scent. Blue, pink, white and yellow flower spikes will bring you colour and fragrance in the middle of winter in the coldest greenhouse.

How to plant

One bulb to a 10-cm (4-in) pot, or three bulbs to a 20-cm (8-in) bowl. Use JIP 1 with one quarter its bulk of sharp sand added to provide rapid drainage, or bulb fibre which should be soaked and squeezed before use. Leave the tops of the bulbs exposed and plant only those of the same variety in each container to ensure that they flower at the same time. Water the bulbs in after planting.
When to plant September and October

How to grow

Plunge the planted bowls or pots outdoors under peat or sand for eight weeks, then move them into an unheated greenhouse or garden frame. The house can be kept cold (in which case the bulbs will flower rather later), or it may be heated to 7°C (45°F) as soon as the flower buds can be seen. Water carefully and avoid splashing the leaves and flowers. As the flower spikes extend, thin but strong wire can be pushed through them and into the compost for support (see page 56). The pots and bowls can be brought indoors when the bulbs flower if you like, and returned to the garden frame to dry off slowly when the flowers fade.

Plant them out in the garden for colour the following year.

Good varieties

City of Haarlem, yellow, L'Innocence, white; Jan Bos, deep pink; Pink Pearl, pink; Ostara, blue. 'Prepared' bulbs have been specially treated to flower earlier in the first year.

Narcissus

Although we usually call the small-trumpeted and cluster-flowered types 'narcissi', the name really applies to daffodils too. The colour range becomes larger every year.

Yellow, orange or white double and single varieties are now common, but green- and pink-flowered varieties are also appearing – at a price! Once the flowers have faded none of the bulbs are wasted as they can be planted in the garden.

How to plant

Three or four good-sized bulbs will fit in a 15-cm (6-in) pot, or two layers of bulbs can be planted in a 20-cm (8-in) pot. Use JIP 2 with one quarter its bulk of sharp sand added for rapid drainage. Leave the 'noses' of the top layer of bulbs exposed and water them in well.
When to plant Late August to October.

Narcissus **Cragford**

How to grow

Plunge the pots outdoors under peat or sand for eight weeks, then transfer them to a cold greenhouse or garden frame. Push pieces of brushwood among the plants to support them, or position three canes around the sides of the pot and link them together with soft twine. Water when necessary. A little heat may be applied to bring the temperature up to 7°C (45°F). Bring indoors if required when the blooms start to open.

Good varieties

Carlton, 45 cm (18 in), yellow 'daffodil'; Paper White, 45 cm (18 in), clusters of small, white, scented blooms for Christmas; Soleil d'Or, 45 cm (18 in), clusters of bright yellow, scented blooms for Christmas; W. P. Milner, 25 cm

(10 in), creamy white; February Gold, 30 cm (12 in), long yellow trumpet, reflexed 'petals'; Cragford, 45 cm (18 in), white with orange cup; Van Sion, 35 cm (15 in), double yellow.

Tulip

Short or tall, single or double, tulips in shades of red, orange, yellow, pink, mauve, dark brown and white will bring added brilliance to your spring greenhouse bulb display.

How to plant

Set the bulbs quite close together in bowls of fibre or pots of JIP 1 with one quarter its volume of sharp sand added. Five or six bulbs will fit in a 12-cm (5-in) half-pot or pot. Leave the tips of the bulbs showing above the compost and water them in.
When to plant September to November.

How to grow

Plunge the pots or bowls outdoors in sand or peat for eight weeks then bring them into an unheated greenhouse or garden frame and water when dry. When the flower buds have formed the temperature can be increased to 10°C (50°F) if you want to hurry the blooms along. Bring indoors when the blooms open and afterwards plant the bulbs in the garden for future enjoyment.

Good varieties

Peach Blossom, 30 cm (12 in), double pink; Maréchal Niel, 30 cm (12 in), double orange-yellow; Brilliant Star, 30 cm (12 in), single scarlet; Bellona, 35 cm (15 in), single yellow; Stresa, 20 cm (8 in), red and yellow; Cassini, 35 cm (15 in) deep mahogany red; First Lady, 45 cm (18 in), violet purple; Jewel Dance, 30 cm (12 in), carmine, edged with white.

Foliage pot plants

Flowers must be shown off against a suitable background if they are to look their best, and no background is more effective than foliage. Bold or feathery, green or coloured, upright or trailing; somewhere you will always be able to find a plant whose leaves will provide the right effect.

Plants grown for their foliage have one great advantage over those raised for flowers: they are of interest all the year round. It is only necessary to keep your greenhouse frost free to enjoy the delicate tracery of asparagus ferns and the silk oak, the boldly marked leaves of *Begonia rex* and the prayer plant, and the bright colours of the coleus.

Many of these plants can be raised from seeds, others can be divided or propagated from cuttings. All of them are easy to grow once you know their individual preferences which are explained on the following pages.

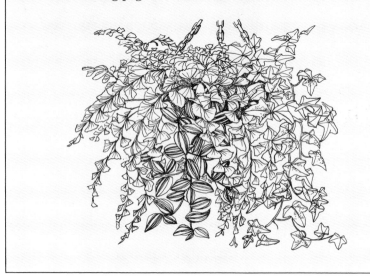

A collection of foliage pot plants provides
an endless variety of colour and texture
throughout the year.

Abutilon

Abutilon striatum thompsonii and
Abutilon savitzii

These two particular abutilons
(sometimes known as Indian
mallows) are particularly noted for
their foliage. *Abutilon striatum
thompsonii* has maple-like leaves
covered in a superb green and
yellow mosaic pattern. Orange, red-
veined bells are carried in summer
and the plant will reach a height of
2 m (6 ft) or more if you let it but
pinching will keep it smaller.
Abutilon savitzii is unlikely to grow
quite as high. It has a more bushy
habit and the leaves are variegated
cream and green. Seeds of various
mixed hybrids are available.

How to start
Cuttings of young shoots can be
rooted in a propagator in summer.
Seeds can be sown in spring.
Sowing temperature 16 to 18°C (60 to
65°F)
Rooting temperature 18°C (65°F)
Growing-on temperature 7°C (45°F)
winter minimum.

How to grow
Pot up the young plants into 8-cm
(3-in) pots of JIP 1 and pot on into
larger containers of JIP 2 as they
grow. Pinch when a few inches high
to encourage bushiness, and
continue to pinch sideshoots after
several leaves have formed. Water
when dry and feed fortnightly in
summer. Keep an eye open for
whitefly and fumigate when
necessary. The plants can be bedded
out in the garden in summer.
Discard when too large to house.

Asparagus ferns

Asparagus plumosus and *Asparagus
sprengeri*

These are not really ferns, but are
so called because of their feathery
leaves. Plumosus is often used with
carnations in buttonholes for
weddings, and sprengeri is its

coarser relative. Plumosus will
climb, unless you have the lower-
growing form *nanus*, and sprengeri
will trail in a foamy cascade which
makes it an ideal plant for a hanging
basket.

How to start
Sow seeds in spring or summer and
divide mature plants at the same
time.
Sowing temperature 18°C (65°F)
Growing-on temperature 7°C (45°F)
winter minimum.

How to grow
Pot up the seedlings or divisions in
8-cm (3-in) and 10-cm (4-in) pots
respectively. Use JIP 1 or a soilless
equivalent and pot on into 12-cm
(5-in) pots of JIP 2 or equivalent
when the plants outgrow their
smaller containers. Provide the
climbing form, plumosus, with
horizontal wire supports. Water

Asparagus plumosus

freely during the summer and feed
fortnightly. Keep a lookout for scale
insects and spray when necessary.
Divide or discard the plants when
they become too large or straggly.

Begonia

Begonia rex

The bold maroon-, silver-, green-,
and brown-variegated leaves of
Begonia rex are held close together to
make mounds of colour. Many
different variegations are available,
some of them quite spectacular.
Large as their pointed leaves are, the

The colourful leaves of *Begonia rex*

plants will not grow much more
than 30 cm (1 ft) high. Pink or white
flowers are carried but they are
insignificant compared to the leaves.

How to start
Take leaf cuttings in summer and
root them in a propagator.
Rooting temperature 16°C (60°F)
Growing-on temperature 10°C (50°F)
winter minimum.

How to grow
Pot up the young plants individually
in 8-cm (3-in) pots of soilless
compost as soon as they are large
enough to handle. Pot on into 12-cm
(5-in) pots when the first containers
are outgrown. Keep warm and
shade from bright sunshine. These
plants grow happily standing under
the greenhouse staging. Feed
fortnightly in summer and water
when dry. Damp down the floor
around the plants daily.

Coleus

This plant's little-used name of
'flame-nettle' tells all. The nettle-like
leaves may be splashed with yellow,
green, white, magenta, crimson,
cerise, dark brown – almost any
colour except blue. A packet of
seeds can bring you untold
variations in leaf form and brilliance,
and the plants will grow to between
30 and 60 cm (1 and 2 ft) high.

How to start
Sow seeds of mixed or single-
coloured hybrid varieties in spring;

Mixed varieties of coleus

take cuttings of named varieties in spring and early summer and root in pots or a propagator.
Sowing temperature 18°C (65°F)
Rooting temperature 16 to 18°C (60 to 65°F)
Growing-on temperature 10°C (50°F) winter minimum.

How to grow

Pot up seedlings into 8-cm (3-in) pots of JIP 1 or a soilless equivalent as soon as you can see which ones have the best colouring. Pot up cuttings when they are rooted. Pinch out the plants when they are 8 or 10 cm (3 or 4 in) high and continue to pinch sideshoots after a few leaves have formed to encourage bushiness. Pot on into 10-cm (4-in) pots of JIP 2 or equivalent as the plants grow. Remove any flower spikes that appear; the stems will become spindly if they are left on. Keep the plants in good light, damp down daily, water well in summer and feed once a week. If you cannot maintain a temperature of 10°C (50°F) discard plants at the end of the season and raise new stock from seed each spring. Overwintered plants may reach a height of 60 cm (2 ft) in 12-cm (5-in) pots.

Good varieties

Mixed strains of *Coleus blumei* will always produce interesting plants. Carefree and Fashion Parade are two more compact-growing mixtures.

Ivy

Hedera varieties

The varieties of *Hedera helix* make superb trailers for hanging baskets, shelves and the front of greenhouse staging. Some have plain green leaves, others are variegated with cream and yellow and one or two varieties are crinkled or frilled around the edges.

Hedera helix Glacier

How to start

Stem cuttings can be rooted in a propagator in spring or summer.
Rooting temperature 16°C (60°F)
Growing-on temperature Will survive in an unheated greenhouse; they are frost hardy.

How to grow

Pot up the rooted cuttings in 8-cm (3-in) pots of JIP 1. Keep cool at all times and water when dry. Shade from bright sunshine and damp down around them in summer. Pinch out shoot tips to encourage branching. Feed fortnightly in summer. Pot on into 10-cm (4-in) pots of JIP 1 as the plants grow. Look out for greenfly and red spider mite and spray when necessary.

Good varieties

Glacier, green and white; Gold Heart, green with central yellow blotch; Brokamp, green becoming bronze in winter; Buttercup, yellow, becoming green as the leaves age; Sagittaefolia, spiky, fingered leaves of green; Cristata, green with crinkled edges.

Pilea

These compact foliage plants can be relied on to provide a varied show of leaf form and colour in a cool greenhouse.

How to start

Stem cuttings can be rooted in a propagator in spring or summer.
Rooting temperature 16°C (60°F)
Growing-on temperature 7°C (45°F) winter minimum.

How to grow

Pot up rooted cuttings in 8-cm (3-in) pots of JIP 1 or a soilless equivalent. Pot on into 10-cm (4-in) containers later. Pinch out shoot tips at 8 cm (3 in) to encourage bushiness. Water thoroughly when dry in summer; more sparingly in winter. Shade from strong sunshine must be provided. Feed fortnightly in summer.

Good varieties
Pilea cadierei nana, aluminium plant, 23 cm (9 in), dark green leaves marked with silver grey; *Pilea microphylla*, artillery plant, 15 cm (6 in), ferny leaves and minute flowers which expel their pollen in clouds if disturbed; *Pilea* Moon Valley, 23 cm (9 in), deeply veined green and bronze leaves; *Pilea* Silvertree, 23 cm (9 in), oval bronze leaves decorated with silver herringbones.

Prayer plant

Maranta varieties

The marantas are a beautiful but rather temperamental group of plants with very pronounced likes and dislikes. Even so they are stunning when well grown and therefore worth a little perseverance. Only one species is the true prayer plant which folds up its leaves at night.

How to start
Divide mature plants in spring.
Growing-on temperature 13°C (55°F) winter minimum. Keep warm in summer.

How to grow
Pot up the divisions (which should have as much root as possible) in 10-cm (4-in) pots of soilless compost, or a mixture of soilless and JIP 1 compost. Marantas like a moisture-retentive medium but one which is 'open' and not likely to become compacted. Grow in shady conditions (under the greenhouse staging if you like) and water them when they are dry. Feed fortnightly in summer and damp down around the plants. Keep the compost fairly dry in winter.

Good varieties
Maranta leuconeura kerchoveana, prayer plant, 23 cm (9 in), pale green leaves marked with brown; *Maranta leuconeura erythrophylla*, pale green leaves marked with dark green and bright red.

The graceful spider plant (*Chlorophytum comosum variegatum*)

Silk oak

Grevillea robusta

An elegant and stately plant for a cool greenhouse. Arching ferny leaves of dark green (red-brown when young) are carried symmetrically up the stem. A packet of this plant's seeds is an excellent buy.

How to start
Sow seeds in spring and summer.
Sowing temperature 18 to 20°C (65 to 70°F)
Growing-on temperature 7°C (45°F) winter minimum.

How to grow
Pot up the seedlings in 8-cm (3-in) pots of JIP 1 as soon as they are large enough to handle. Pot on the plants in JIP 2 as soon as they fill each container. They may eventually be given 25-cm (10-in) pots – if you have room. If you want a branching specimen pinch out the growing point when the plant is 30 cm (12 in) high. Water well and feed every week in summer. Ventilate freely; if kept too hot the plants will shed their leaves. Keep the compost fairly dry in winter. Discard when too large to be accommodated.

Spider plant

Chlorophytum comosum variegatum

One of the most popular house plants of all time, the spider plant is highly decorative in the greenhouse too. The bright green- and cream-striped fountains of leaves will look good on shelves, under the staging or tumbling from hanging baskets. The plantlets carried on long arching stems create great interest and are valuable for propagation.

How to start
Plantlets can be rooted in jars of water or 8-cm (3-in) pots of JIP 1 or a soilless compost at any time of year. Divide mature plants in spring.
Growing-on temperature 7°C (45°F) winter minimum.

How to grow
Tolerant of sun or shade, the spider

plant is easy to grow provided that it always has a large enough pot and some good compost. Pot it on frequently in JIP 2 or a soilless equivalent and water it well through summer but more sparingly in winter. Feed every week from June to September. Starved plants will become weak and their leaf tips will turn brown. Divide or discard plants when they become too large for the space available.

Wandering Jew

Tradescantia varieties

The Wandering Jew, or tradescantia, is one of the easiest plants to grow. Like roses, tradescantias grow in spite of their owners rather than because of them. Trailing stems clad in oval leaves of green and cream, green and white, or even green and pink, are produced in abundance. The plants look best in hanging baskets or where their stems can be allowed to dangle over the edge of shelves and staging.

How to start
Dib stem cuttings into pots of JIP 1 or a soilless equivalent, then simply water and leave to grow.
Rooting temperature 13 to 16°C (55 to 60°F)
Growing-on temperature 7°C (45°F) winter minimum.

How to grow
Pot on when necessary into containers of JIP 1 or a soilless equivalent. Water well in summer and feed the plants fortnightly to keep them in the peak of condition. They will always survive but if kept dry and starved some of their leaves will dry off. Sun or light shade suits them, but in very dark corners their variegation will fade.

Good varieties
Tradescantia fluminensis is available in several forms; one of the best is Quicksilver, green and white.

Climbers and border plants

If you're fortunate enough to have a large greenhouse with plenty of headroom you can enjoy flowers of stature by planting climbers or shrubs in the border soil and training their stems on wires suspended from the rafters. This need not stop you from growing plants on staging; the main stems of the climbers can be taken up behind the bench. You can either plant them when they are small and put the staging in position when they have grown above its level, or else plant larger specimens that will be taller at the outset.

If you don't have a border you can plant in tubs or large pots, standing these on the staging if you wish. In a lean-to the climbers can be planted in a raised or ground-level border against the back wall and trained up wires or trelliswork.

Even small greenhouses can accommodate a climber if the plant is properly positioned. The annual types in particular will be some time before they fill their allotted space, and so will allow adequate light penetration when bedding plants are being raised in spring. They will also provide natural shade when it is wanted in summer.

The selection of climbers and border plants on the following pages will provide scent and colour in winter and summer.

The beautiful passion flower is just one of
the impressive climbers which you can
grow in your greenhouse border.

Bottle brush tree

Callistemon species

Highly decorative evergreen shrubs
which wreathe their stems with
scarlet 'bottle brush' plumes in late
spring or summer.

How to start
Cuttings of firm growths can be
rooted in a propagator in summer,
potted up and on in JIP 1 and 2 until
large enough to be planted out.
Rooting temperature 18°C (65°F)
Growing-on temperature 7°C (45°F)
winter minimum.

Planting
Plant in spring in tubs or large pots
of JIP 2, or in a sunny greenhouse
border enriched with compost or
manure and a little general fertilizer.

How to grow
Ventilate well at all times. Water
freely in summer, more sparingly in
winter – just enough to keep the
compost moist. Feed fortnightly in
summer. Repot or topdress plants
grown in tubs or pots every other
spring.
Pruning and training Tie in the
branches to support wires spaced at
30-cm (12-in) intervals on the rear
wall of a lean-to or the rafters of
span-roof houses. Prune only when
the plant is outgrowing its allotted
space and then shorten the

Callistemon citrinus splendens

Bougainvillea Poultens Special

sideshoots after flowering.

Good varieties
Callistemon citrinus splendens, 2 m
(6 ft); *Callistemon linearis*, 1.25 m
(4 ft), better for small greenhouses;
Callistemon speciosus, 3 m (10 ft), for
large greenhouses only.

Bougainvillea

Anyone who has visited the
Mediterranean will come back with
indelible memories of this vividly
coloured plant. The flowers are
small and white but the bracts that
surround them are cerise, magenta,
orange, rosy purple or white,
providing a brilliant show in
summer.

How to start
Stem cuttings can be rooted in a
propagator in summer and grown
on in JIP 2 compost until large
enough to plant out. Plants will
need cane supports when in pots.
Rooting temperature 20°C (70°F)
Growing-on temperature 7 to 10°C (45
to 50°F) winter minimum.

Planting
Plant in spring in tubs or large pots
of JIP 2, or in a sunny greenhouse
border enriched with compost or
manure and fertilizer.

How to grow
Water freely in summer and
sparingly in winter to keep the soil
fairly dry. Spray the foliage daily in
summer with rainwater. Ventilate
well in warm weather. Feed
fortnightly when in bloom. Repot
or topdress container-grown plants
annually in spring.
Pruning and training Tie in the
branches to support wires and cut
back the sideshoots to three or four
buds in early spring. Remove any
over-long or weak shoots at the
same time.

Good varieties
Bougainvillea buttiana, 3 m (10 ft),
smaller if pruned back, deep red,
and variety Orange King, orange.
Bougainvillea glabra, 2 m (6 ft), cerise,
and varieties Snow White, creamy
white; Magnifica, rosy purple.

Camellia

Popular as garden shrubs, camellias
can be enjoyed even more in a cool
greenhouse where their flowers will
be untouched by frost. Double or
single red, pink, mauve and white
varieties are available, as well as
some with striped blooms. They
flower in late winter and spring.

How to start

Cuttings of firm young shoots can be rooted in a propagator or under mist in summer.
Rooting temperature 16 to 18°C (60 to 65°F)
Growing-on temperature An unheated greenhouse suits them well. Keep cool in summer.

Planting

Plant in autumn in tubs of JIP ericaceous mix (which is lime free), or border soil enriched with peat and a little garden compost or manure.

How to grow

The soil around camellias must never be allowed to dry out or they will lose their flower buds as well as their leaves. Water freely in summer and winter whenever the soil shows the slightest signs of dryness. Two or three applications of diluted iron sequestrene (a tonic containing magnesium) will work wonders if applied at monthly intervals in summer. Ventilate and shade well in summer to keep the plants cool.

Camellia Golden Spangles

Topdress tub-grown plants annually after flowering. Border-grown plants will appreciate an annual mulch of well-rotted manure or garden compost in spring. Spray the foliage daily with rainwater in summer.
Pruning and training Tie in the stems to horizontal wires to make a well-spaced framework. Prune out unwanted and weak shoots after flowering.

Good varieties

Camellia japonica provides us with some of the best varieties and these include: Adolphe Audusson, semi-double, rich red; Alba Plena, double white; Apple Blossom, semi-double, pink; Contessa Lavinia Maggi, white with rose stripes; Peach Blossom, semi-double, pale pink. All will grow to 2 or 3 m (6 or 10 ft) high.

Cup and saucer vine

Cobaea scandens

When grown outdoors this plant has to be treated as an annual because it is killed by the first frosts. If grown in a frost-free greenhouse though, it will survive from year to year, producing its quaint white to purple flowers for most of the summer.

How to start

Seeds can be sown in spring and the young plants potted up in containers of JIP 1 or a soilless equivalent. Cuttings of young shoots can be rooted in a propagator in summer.
Sowing temperature 16°C (60°F)
Rooting temperature 18°C (65°F)
Growing-on temperature 7°C (45°F)

Planting

Plant in early summer in large pots or tubs of JIP 2 or in sunny greenhouse borders. No soil enrichment is necessary as this may lead to excessive leaf growth.

How to grow

Water freely in summer and feed occasionally. Ventilate well in warm spells. Spray the plant with rainwater daily in summer. Topdress container-grown plants in spring.
Pruning and training Tie the main stems to horizontal wires or trelliswork; the new stems will cling by themselves with the aid of tendrils. Cut back the sideshoots in February to three or four buds.

Jasmine

Jasminum polyanthum and Jasminum primulinum

Two dainty climbers with delightful flowers. Polyanthum bears clusters

of scented, white, starry blooms in spring and early summer, and primulinum (more correctly known as *Jasminum mesnyi*) has larger blooms of primrose yellow in winter. Both will grow to a height of 2 or 3 m (6 or 10 ft).

Jasminum polyanthum

How to start

Short sideshoots can be removed with a heel in spring and rooted in a propagator. Pot up in JIP 1 or a soilless equivalent until the plants are large enough to be planted out.
Rooting temperature 16°C (60°F)
Growing-on temperature 7°C (45°F) winter minimum.

Planting

Plant in early spring in large pots or tubs of JIP 2 or in sunny borders enriched with a little well-rotted garden compost or manure.

How to grow

Ventilate well in warm weather and spray the foliage with rainwater daily in summer. Feed occasionally; too much food will produce leaves at the expense of flowers. Water freely in summer, more sparingly in winter. Topdress pot- or tub-grown plants annually in spring.
Pruning and training Tie the stems to horizontal wires or loop them through trelliswork. Prune out any overcrowding growths after flowering, and shorten any rampant shoots through the summer.

Mimosa

Acacia dealbata

The florist's mimosa is a delightful, if space-consuming plant for a cool greenhouse. Its foliage is green and feathery and its fluffy, bright yellow flowers appear on established plants in spring. The stems will reach 6 m (20 ft) or more if you let them, but the plant can easily be kept in check by careful pruning.

How to start

Heel cuttings can be rooted in a propagator in summer but it is easier to raise the plants from seeds sown in spring. Pot up the plants in JIP ericaceous compost until they are ready to be planted out.
Sowing temperature 18°C (65°F)
Rooting temperature 18°C (65°F)
Growing-on temperature 7°C (45°F) winter minimum.

Planting

Plant in spring in pots or tubs of JIP ericaceous mix, or in a sunny border enriched with well-rotted manure, garden compost or peat.

How to grow

Water freely in summer when dry, more sparingly in winter, but never allow the soil to dry out. Ventilate well in summer and spray the foliage daily with rainwater. Topdress plants in tubs and pots each year in spring. Apply a mulch of well-rotted manure at the same time to plants growing in soil borders.
Pruning and training Thin out the shoots immediately after flowering to keep the plant in check. Tie in the main branches to horizontal wires attached to the rafters.

Morning glory

Ipomoea tricolor and *Ipomoea rubro-coerulea*

Quite breathtaking blue trumpet flowers are produced on this annual during the summer. Make sure you see them early; by about 3 o'clock the flowers on most varieties will have closed, never to open again. There are different coloured varieties but none so lovely as the blue.

How to start

Sow the seeds in spring – one to an 8-cm (3-in) pot.
Sowing temperature 18°C (65°F)

Ipomoea tricolor Heavenly Blue

Growing-on temperature 16°C (60°F) in the early stages. No heat needed in late spring and summer.

Planting

Set out the plants in a sunny border or in large pots of JIP 2 or a soilless equivalent in late spring or early summer.

How to grow

Give occasional liquid feeds and water freely in summer. Ventilate well in warm spells.
Pruning and training Allow the stems to twine around a tripod of tall canes or up trelliswork. No pruning is necessary; the plant is discarded in winter and raised afresh from seed each spring.

Good varieties

Heavenly Blue (the best, in my opinion), mid-blue with a white throat; Scarlet O'Hara, rosy red; Flying Saucers, blue and white striped; Early Call Rose, rose pink and white, stays open slightly longer. All will reach a height of 3 m (10 ft) in a season but can be pinched back a little to keep them smaller.

Passion flower

Passiflora caerulea

A vigorous evergreen climber with hand-shaped leaves and intriguing flowers which are said to depict the passion of Christ. *Passiflora caerulea* has white and blue flowers in summer, and its variety Constance Elliott has plain white blooms of a

Mimosa (acacia)

larger size. Both these plants are very vigorous and will cover whatever space you provide. Orange egg-shaped fruits are produced in good summers and these are edible but rather pippy.

How to start
Cuttings of shoot tips will root in a propagator in summer. Pot up and grow on in JIP 1 when rooted.
Rooting temperature 18°C (65°F)
Growing-on temperature The plant is hardy and will survive most winters in an unheated greenhouse.

Planting
Plant in spring in a sunny border enriched with a little well-rotted compost or manure; too much nutrition will produce leaves rather than flowers. The plant will also grow in large pots or tubs of JIP 2.

How to grow
Water freely in summer and just sufficiently to keep the soil moist in winter. Feed occasionally through the summer and ventilate well at all times. Spray the leaves daily in warm weather with rainwater. Topdress plants being grown in pots each spring.
Pruning and training Remove any weak or badly placed shoots as soon as they are seen. The main pruning is carried out in winter, when the shoots are thinned out to a manageable framework and any unwanted stems cut back to leave two or three buds. Tie in all the stems retained to a trellis framework or horizontal wires.

Stephanotis

Perhaps most frequently seen in wedding bouquets, *Stephanotis floribunda* is an evergreen climber with deliciously scented flowers which appear in late spring and summer. It will eventually reach a height of 3 m (10 ft) or so.

How to start
Cuttings of firm young growths can be rooted in a propagator in spring. Pot up the young rooted plants in JIP ericaceous mix and grow them on before planting out.

Rooting temperature 18°C (65°F)
Growing-on temperature 13°C (55°F)

Planting
Plant in spring in border soil free of lime and enriched with peat; or plant in tubs or large pots of JIP ericaceous mix.

How to grow
Feed fortnightly from May to September and water well when dry. Shade from bright sunshine in summer and spray daily with rainwater. Keep the compost just moist in winter. Topdress container-grown plants in spring.

Stephanotis floribunda

Pruning and training No regular pruning is needed but remove badly placed or unwanted shoots in winter. Tie the main stems to horizontal wires or trelliswork.

Wax plant

Hoya carnosa

The rather ungainly twining stems of this plant are amply made up for by the clusters of white, maroon-centred flowers which are carried in summer. Both the leaves and the flowers have a waxy appearance which gave rise to its common name. If you see a clear drop of liquid hanging from a bloom, taste it – it's just like honey. The plant will produce 3-m (10-ft) stems with ease, but these can be trained over and around the supports to take up less room.

CLIMBERS AND
BORDER PLANTS

How to start
Suitable stems can be layered in spring or summer; cuttings of firm young growths can be rooted in a propagator in summer. Pot up the young plants in JIP 1 or a soilless equivalent when roots have formed.
Rooting temperature 20°C (70°F)
Growing-on temperature 7 to 10°C (45 to 50°F) winter minimum. Keep warm in summer.

Planting
Plant in spring in pots or tubs of JIP 2 or in soil borders enriched with a little well-rotted compost or manure.

How to grow
Ventilate in warm weather and shade the plants from strong summer sunshine. Water freely in spring and summer, but keep the compost only just moist in autumn and winter. Spray the leaves with rainwater daily in hot weather and feed fortnightly with a liquid fertilizer throughout the summer. Keep an eye open for mealy bug and scale insects, spraying if attacks are severe.
Pruning and training Remove only those growths which are weak or badly placed, cutting them out in winter. Do not cut off old flower stalks as these will carry more blooms later. Train the stems around horizontal wires or trelliswork, tying them in if necessary with soft twine.

Wax plant (*Hoya carnosa*)

Plants for specialists

For most of us the greenhouse must serve as home for a wide variety of plants. We try to grow heat-loving cucumbers and melons alongside pots of geraniums in summer, and maybe crops of winter lettuce with cyclamen, cinerarias and freesias – all with varying degrees of success. However, there are gardeners who have a passion for one particular kind of plant to which they are prepared to devote all their greenhouse space; they may even invest in a second greenhouse and enjoy the best of both worlds.

Without doubt, plants of one kind which have a greenhouse to themselves do grow better because conditions can be tailored exactly to their requirements. If you can't go this far but want to grow a good range of one particular kind of plant why not partition off one end of your greenhouse and devote it solely to their culture? A permanent timber and glass dividing wall is one solution; a temporary timber and polythene screen is another – both can be fitted with doors to allow access.

The following is an introduction to a few of the most popular 'special groups' to which you might become addicted. You won't become an expert overnight but I hope these brief notes will whet your appetite.

A striking and unusual effect can be
created with a specialist collection of one
type of plant.

Alpines

Rock plants may seem to be a strange choice for a greenhouse. Certainly there are many types for which such protection is totally unnecessary, but some plants from alpine regions are not at all happy in our gardens because our winters are too wet. In their native regions they are used to a warm, dry blanket of snow.

In the sheltered environment of the alpine house they will be happier: the flowers may well last longer, and they will be easier to see at close quarters too. Dwarf conifers in pots can provide a permanent background to the display.

The plants will not need to stay in the house all the year round. If a plunge bed is available they can be kept in the greenhouse for their season of glory and moved outdoors into the cool, moist medium for the summer.

Special alpine houses are available but an ordinary span-roof greenhouse will grow the plants just as well provided that it is fitted with plenty of ventilators – under the staging as well as in the sides and roof if possible.

Ventilation is very important, the plants will need all they can get in summer. In winter they will need a constant supply of air but no draughts; always ventilate cautiously on the leeward side of the house.

Shading will be needed in periods of bright sunshine from about April onwards; blinds are best but whitewash compound can also be used.

The staging in an alpine house is traditionally covered with shingle which looks good and allows free drainage of moisture from the pots. The alpine house requires no heating which is an added bonus.

Compost
Alpine enthusiasts argue increasingly over the wisdom, or otherwise, of using John Innes compost. Some swear by it, others swear at it. If you decide to use it, add about one

quarter its volume of fine grit or coarse sand because alpines demand very rapid drainage. If you side with those who say it is too rich and makes the plants grow too lush, try a mixture of equal parts loam, leafmould or peat, and coarse sand. Like all plants, alpines should be potted on when they outgrow their containers, though this may not be every year.

Cover the surface of the compost with a layer of fine grit which shows off the plants and prevents mud-splashing.

Containers
Most alpines have a shallow root system and are happy in half pots or the wider 'pans'. Clay containers are used traditionally but plastic ones are just as good provided that you water them a little less frequently. Coarse chippings or crocks in the base of all containers will get excess water away quickly.

Watering
In spring and summer when they are growing, alpines require a good supply of water. Weigh plastic containers in your hand to test them; rap clay ones with your knuckle or a wooden cotton reel stuck to the end of a garden cane.

In winter keep the compost on the dry side and water when necessary in the morning so that the plants are free of water droplets by the evening. Keep water off the leaves.

Propagation
Seeds, cuttings and division are the three main means of increase. Sow seeds in gritty compost, cover lightly, and keep in a cool shady frame. Cuttings, too, will need no heat – they can be inserted outdoors or in a frame.

Descriptive catalogues are available from several specialist nurseries and some of them are listed on page 122.

Cacti

Natives of countries which are for the most part hot and dry, cacti and other succulents have adapted themselves remarkably well to cope with extremes of climate. Large and small types are available in many different forms and lots of them have brilliantly coloured flowers.

The distinction between cacti and other succulents is a simple one: cacti belong to the plant family *Cactaceae*; many of them have spines and very fat stems with no leaves. Other succulents differ botanically and so are classified separately but they still have fleshy leaves and stems which are capable of storing water. From this you will see that all cacti are succulents, but not all succulents are cacti.

A look at the natural environment of the plants gives some idea of what they will require in cultivation. They are natives of hot areas with high light intensity and so need as much sun as possible. Infrequent rain is made full use of – the plants store the moisture in their fleshy leaves and stems so that during long periods of drought they can draw on their internal moisture reserves.

Type of greenhouse
An ordinary span-roof or lean-to of modest size will accommodate a surprisingly large number of plants on staging and shelves. Most succulents grow quite slowly and can be packed closely together provided that they are given good light. Although warmth is essential in summer, so too is fresh air. Make sure that there are enough ventilators to allow good air circulation.

Temperatures and watering
It's natural to think that succulents need heat all the year round, but in winter they can be kept very cool – temperatures being allowed to fall as low as 4°C (40°F). Provided that the compost in the pots is dry the plants will come to no harm. From November to March water can be

A well-tended collection of alpine plants

withheld entirely: this is the plants' resting period. In spring water gradually at first, until eventually the compost is soaked thoroughly every time it is seen to be dry. Temperatures can be allowed to rise naturally from April onwards.

There is always a chance that the succulents could be scorched by bright sunlight when they are grown under glass, so apply a light coating of whitewash-type shading in summer, or invest in some blinds. Ease off watering at the end of the summer as the plants approach their resting season.

Compost

Like alpine growers, cactus experts have their own recipes for success, but JIP 1 with one quarter its volume of fine grit added will provide a nourishing and well-drained medium for these desert natives.

Potting

Unlike most plants cacti do not need potting regularly. Their roots are undemanding and will extend quite slowly. Only pot on the plants when their roots are very restricted; April is the best time for the job.

Propagation

Seeds and division are the most common means of increase, though cuttings can also be taken of many species, and some of the more peculiar (and unsightly) types are grafted.

Ferns

Even though ferns do not produce flowers they are among the most decorative and varied of greenhouse plants. Their fronds, in many shades of green, may be contrastingly marked or delicately fingered, feathery like the maidenhair fern, or thick and glossy like the bird's nest fern. Variety of form is certainly not lacking. Alone they provide a rich green tapestry; mixed with other plants they contrast effectively with vivid blooms.

Type of greenhouse

Any greenhouse is suitable for ferns, provided that it can be protected by one means or another from scorching summer sunlight. North-facing lean-tos are particularly suitable but those of other aspects (and free-standing greenhouses too) can be used if shading is provided in summer.

A selection of delicate ferns

Stout benching equipped with a layer of shingle is perhaps the best form of support as it will retain moisture and keep the atmosphere humid. Some species of fern thrive in fairly dense shade and will do well if placed under the staging.

Temperatures

Ferns vary in their temperature requirements. Some are natives of warm, humid 'jungle' conditions and like to be kept warm; others like it cooler and will happily survive in an unheated greenhouse. Choose the ones you feel you can afford to cater for but in either case ventilate very carefully to avoid harmful, cold draughts.

Potting

Any plants that need a new pot are moved on in spring at the start of the growing season. Clay and plastic pots are both suitable, but ferns with pendulous fronds are seen to best advantage when planted in hanging baskets suspended from the roof of the greenhouse or from brackets which have been firmly fastened to the back wall of a lean-to greenhouse.

Use peat-based composts for potting, or JIP ericaceous mix with one half its own volume of coarse peat added. The experts of old mixed together varying quantities of loam, peat, leafmould, brickdust and sharp sand – experiment with these if you wish, bearing in mind that you are out to produce a well-drained but spongy mixture which will retain adequate moisture.

A range of cacti in a small greenhouse

Watering

From spring until late summer the compost around ferns should be kept quite moist. In winter it can be left just a little dryer but it should never be allowed to dry out completely or the plants will suffer and the compost will be difficult to re-wet. During the growing season (April to September) damp down the floors and staging twice a day to maintain a humid atmosphere.

Feeding need not be carried out with any regularity. A weak dose of diluted liquid fertilizer can be given two or three times through the growing season.

Propagation

Having no flowers, ferns cannot produce seeds, so they produce the next best thing – spores. These are to be found in brown spots on the underside of the fronds and, when ripe, they are shed in quantity. Spores can be germinated on the surface of moist, peaty compost covered with glass to prevent dehydration. The growth of algae and liverworts is always a problem, but they can be kept in check to some extent if the compost is drenched with boiling water a few hours before sowing.

The young plants may take months to emerge but, when large enough, can be pricked out like seedlings.

Division is simpler and a good deal quicker; all ferns that form thick clumps can be increased in this way and potted up in a suitable compost.

Orchids

Don't be put off growing orchids by the mystique that surrounds them. They certainly require rather different culture to other plants, but if their whims are catered for they are not difficult to grow well. Massive or miniature blooms in rainbow colours will give you unending pleasure, for the plants bloom at various times of the year, many of them in winter.

Type of greenhouse

An ordinary well-lit greenhouse, whether free-standing or lean-to, will make a good home for orchids. Ventilation must be adequate, and there must be provision for shading in bright sunshine. Blinds are best because they can be rolled down to protect flowering plants in sudden bursts of bright winter sunshine, and rolled up again when the danger of scorching is past.

Shingle-covered benching is again the most suitable staging because it retains moisture and humidifies the air – orchids thrive in a moist atmosphere. Tiered staging on top of the gravel bench is a good idea too; more plants can be fitted in but the benefit of humidity is still felt.

Orchid *Cattleya* hybrid

Temperatures

There are orchids that prefer a warm environment, and those that like it cool, but for most of them a winter minimum of 13 to 16°C (55 to 60°F) must be maintained. Cymbidiums are one of the largest-flowered and most popular orchids and they will tolerate 7°C (45°F) in winter which is a point in their favour. Ventilate carefully when necessary to avoid creating harmful draughts.

Potting

Orchids start into growth at different times, but it is at this stage that they should be potted on when necessary. A mixture of 3 parts osmunda fibre to 1 part sphagnum moss is the traditional compost mixture, but both materials may be hard to find and orchid growers may be able to offer you a more readily

available mixture. Nylon fibre, bracken fibre and shredded bark have all been used instead of osmunda fibre which is derived from the roots of the royal fern *Osmunda regalis*.

Pack the compost gently round the roots of the plant and ease it into the pot so that all the fibres run from top to bottom. The surface can be trimmed level with the rim of the pot using sheep shears (if you happen to have a pair!) or with short-bladed scissors.

Watering

Orchids will need a plentiful supply of water in the growing season, soak the compost whenever it shows signs of drying out. Ease off in winter but do not allow the compost to become comply dry. Damp down the greenhouse path and staging twice a day in spring and summer, and on sunny days in autumn and winter.

Propagation

Seeds of orchids are rather difficult to germinate in the usual way, and so are usually raised on sterile nutrient solutions in flasks and test tubes. This may be just the sort of thing you enjoy but if it isn't, stick to division as the most reliable means of propagation and split the plants you want to increase in spring.

Orchid *Cymbidium* hybrid

Fruit

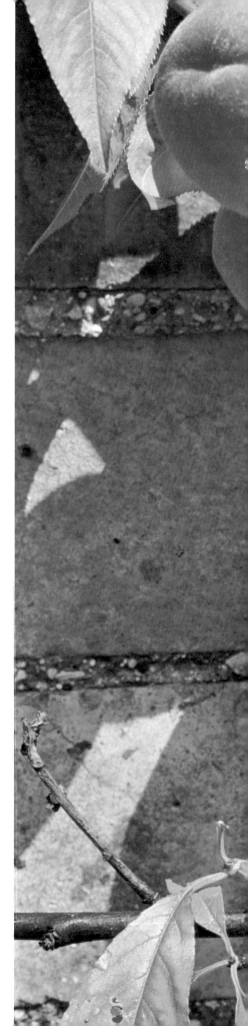

There's something very satisfying in beating the elements and producing succulent fruits that are difficult or impossible to grow in the garden. With just a little heat you can enjoy many of these crops several weeks in advance of their normal season – just when they are at their highest price in the shops. You'll have had to pay for the heat to raise them, and you might not be saving any money, but when you sink your teeth into that first peach or melon and the juice runs down your chin, you will convince yourself that no shop-bought fruit ever tasted so good!

You'll need a little room to grow peaches, nectarines and grapes and they will be permanent residents with their roots in the ground and their stems trained to wires. Melons and strawberries however can usually be fitted into the smallest greenhouse and will take up space for only part of the year.

If you make room for at least one of these crops you will find that the trouble involved in growing it is more than compensated for at harvest time.

For details of pests and diseases see pages 112 to 117.

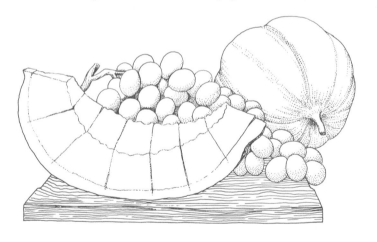

Delicious peaches can be grown
against the back wall of a lean-to greenhouse.

96

Grapes

You do need a little room for a grape vine and I suggest that you don't consider planting one unless your greenhouse is at least 3.5 m (12 ft) long. You can always resort to growing vines in pots if you lack space; details are given for this.

Preparing the soil

The traditional way of growing vines involved planting them outside the greenhouse and training their stems through a hole made in the greenhouse wall. Fortunately this idea has died out. It is far easier to control feeding and watering of the vine when it is planted inside.

To start with, you will need a good piece of border soil in which the vine can sink its roots. Dig the border to a depth of two spits. This involves digging out the first spade's depth (spit) of soil, forking the layer underneath and returning the topsoil. Work two bucketfuls of well-rotted compost or manure and a 10-cm (4-in) potful of general fertilizer into each square metre (yard) of the top spit. If drainage is not very good the soil should be removed to a depth of 60 cm (2 ft) and a 15-cm (6-in) layer of rubble deposited in the base before the soil is returned.

Before you plant fix training wires to the rafters of the greenhouse, spacing them at 35-cm (15-in) intervals and supporting them 20 cm (8 in) away from the framework with metal vine eyes.

Which variety?

Expert growers will tell you that the finest variety of all is Muscat of Alexandria. This may be true but the sad fact is that this variety does not fruit well unless it has plenty of heat. Play safe by planting Black Hamburgh if you want a black grape, or Royal Muscadine if you prefer the yellow/green variety. These two are very tasty and far less temperamental than their high class relative.

Planting

Dormant bare-root vines can be

A grape vine in a small greenhouse

planted from November to March; container-grown specimens at any time of year. Take out a hole which is large enough to accommodate all the roots when they are spread out (or the rootball if the vine is container grown) and after planting firm the soil back into place with your foot. Plant so that the stem is 15 cm (6 in) or so from the side of the greenhouse and check that the soil level corresponds with the old soil mark on the stem of the vine. The roots should be 10 to 15 cm (4 to 6 in) below the surface.

Pruning and training

There are several ways of training vines, but the following is the simplest and most effective. Once the vine is planted shorten the main rod to 60 cm (2 ft). As the buds start to grow, rub out all but the topmost shoot and train this upwards towards the ridge of the house, pinching out its tip when it is 2 m (6 ft) long. Support the shoot by fastening it to a long cane tied to the training wires. Sideshoots will emerge from the main stem and these may be thinned out to leave one every 35 cm (15 in) to correspond with each wire on the roof. Carefully tie these lateral shoots to the wires and stop them (by pinching out their tips) when they have reached a length of 1 m (3 ft). Sideshoots which emerge from these main laterals can be pinched out after their first leaf.

In the first autumn after planting the main lateral shoots can be cut back to just two buds, and the main stem shortened by two thirds of its length.

In subsequent years one lateral should be allowed to grow from each of these 'spurs' and stopped two or three leaves further on than the flower cluster which it will carry. Each autumn the laterals are cut back equally hard, and the main rod is allowed to put on perhaps 60 cm (2 ft) a year until it is eventually pruned to just below the ridge.

Growing conditions

In winter the greenhouse should be unheated, well ventilated and the vine allowed to rest. The rod is usually untied from the wire

framework and lowered so that it can be brushed free of loose bark and painted with tar oil to kill overwintering pests such as mealy bug, scale insects and red spider mite. It is not necessary to water the soil in winter.

If you can afford to apply heat from January onwards your grapes will mature much more quickly. Close the ventilators and gradually increase the temperature from 7 to 10°C (45 to 50°F) over the first couple of weeks, bringing it up to 16°C (60°F) after about a month. The grapes started in January will be ready to eat in June or July.

In an unheated greenhouse the vine can be started into growth in April and fruits will ripen in August and September.

As soon as you start to apply heat, the border soil around the roots should be given a good soak. Leave the hosepipe running on it for a couple of hours and repeat this treatment when the soil looks as if it is drying out (scrape a few inches away with a trowel to see). Damp down daily. When the shoots begin to grow spray them with tepid rainwater every day until the fruits assume their final colouring.

As soon as vines start to bloom keep them warm at night – 13°C (55°F) is sufficient, and dust the flowers with a rabbit's tail or a fine paintbrush to assist pollination.

Once the shoots are growing away ventilate well at all times without creating draughts: an automatic ventilating arm will be very useful. In summer the average day temperature should be between 15 and 20°C (60 and 70°F), and the night temperature around 13°C (55°F).

Apply a liquid feed to the soil every few weeks until the fruits are almost mature, and shade the developing fruits from strong sunshine with blinds or whitewash compound.

Thinning

If all the fruits are allowed to remain

they will be small and fungus diseases may attack the overcrowded bunch. Working from the bottom to the top of the bunch thin the fruits out when they are the size of peas so that about 1 cm ($\frac{1}{2}$ in) is left between each one and its neighbours. Use pointed scissors to cut out unwanted fruits and do not touch the bunch with your fingers.

Vines in pots

If your greenhouse is too small for a border-planted vine why not consider planting one in a pot? Black Hamburgh and Royal Muscadine can still be used, and a container-grown plant bought from a nursery or garden centre can be transferred to a 30-cm (12-in) pot at any time of year. JIP 3 compost should be used and the roots firmed in well.

Push a 1.5-m (5-ft) cane in at either side of the pot to form a widely spaced 'V', and join them at the top with a piece of stout wire or another cane to make a shape like a large croquet hoop.

The main rod is led around the hoop and a lateral allowed to develop every 30 cm (12 in) or so. Stop the laterals two leaves after the flower truss and allow only half-a-dozen bunches to form. In winter cut back the laterals to two buds and shorten the main rod by half its length.

Pot-grown vines are started into growth in the same way as planted vines and at the same time but they can be placed outside through the winter. Much more attention will have to be paid to watering and feeding – the plants must never be allowed to dry out, and liquid feeds should be given fortnightly from June to September. Topdress in early spring and discard the vines after three or four years.

Harvesting

Cut the bunches of grapes as you want them when they are soft and ripe; this will be about four weeks after they change colour. After harvesting ventilate well and ease

Grape, variety Muscat of Alexandria

off watering so that the vine is slowly eased into dormancy.

Pests, diseases and disorders

Aphids, mealy bug, red spider mite, scalding, scale insects and shanking.

Melons

Even quite small greenhouses can usually accommodate a melon.

Which variety?

If you want large melons choose Emerald Gem, which has green flesh, or Hero of Lockinge, with white flesh. The canteloupe melons are smaller but deliciously sweet and they demand less heat. Sweetheart and Charantais are both good.

Sowing

In March or April sow two seeds in an 8-cm (3-in) peat pot of seed compost and germinate them in a temperature of 18°C (65°F). Remove the weakest seedling after germination and grow on the remaining plant in a temperature of 16°C (60°F).

Planting

Obtain a wooden box 23 cm deep by 30 cm by 60 cm (9 in by 12 in by 24 in) from a friendly greengrocer

and place it on the staging. Fill it to the 15-cm (6-in) mark with JIP 3. Alternatively, use a growing bag.

The shoots of the melon will be trained up wires and these should run horizontally up the roof of the house at 30-cm (1-ft) intervals. Fasten them to 15-cm (6-in) long vine eyes. Plant the young melon so that the rim of its moist peat pot is just below the surface of the compost. Water the plant in and lead its shoot to the wires with a cane.

Training

Grow the main stem straight up,

Stringback melons

pinching out its tip if, or when, it reaches the ridge of the house. Tie this stem loosely to each wire it passes. Pinch all sideshoots out after their second leaf and tie them to the horizontal wires.

Growing conditions

Water the plants well and never allow the compost to dry out. Maintain a night temperature of 16°C (60°F). Spray the plants daily with tepid rainwater and keep the floor and staging damped down to create a humid atmosphere.

Pollinating

When four or five female flowers (the ones with round swellings behind them) open at the same time on different sideshoots, pick off a male flower, remove its petals and dust the pollen on to each of the females. Keep the ventilators closed and the house humid on the day you pollinate, and try to do the job around midday. If any of the pollinated flowers later fall off, remove the others, wait for four more to open simultaneously and, repeat the procedure.

Growing on

Feed every week once the fruits have set and pinch off all but the four or five that were pollinated.

Topdress with JIP 3 when roots can be seen on the surface of the compost. When the fruits are the size of tennis balls they can be supported in nets or string bags slung from the rafters. Shade the plants from strong sunshine and ventilate carefully through the summer.

Harvesting

As soon as the fruits start to smell sweet, ease off watering and keep the soil on the dry side to allow ripening and to prevent the fruits from splitting. The melon will feel soft at the end furthest from the stalk when it is ready for picking. Clear out the plants when they have finished cropping.

Pests, diseases and disorders

Aphids, red spider mite, stem rot and whitefly.

Peaches and Nectarines

The first peach plucked from a healthy, well-trained tree is a landmark in the greenhouse owner's life and a moment to be savoured. In a span-roof greenhouse a peach tree will take up far too much room and exclude a lot of light, but in a

Charentais melons

lean-to greenhouse it can be kept well under control against the rear wall. The nectarine is nothing more than a smooth-skinned peach and can be grown in exactly the same way as its downy relative.

Nectarines

Preparing the soil

At the foot of the lean-to wall dig the soil to a depth of two spits (spade blades), working one bucket of well-rotted manure or garden compost into each square metre (yard) of topsoil. A couple of weeks later, if the soil is not already chalky, give it a dressing of lime at the rate of three or four handfuls to the square metre (yard). As with grapes, place a layer of rubble in the bottom of the trench when the soil is excavated if drainage is likely to be poor.

Which variety?

It is possible to grow your own peach from a stone but personally I prefer a named variety whose fruits I can rely on for size and flavour. Nursery-raised plants are usually propagated by budding (that is, a bud of the peach variety from which fruit is required is inserted in the stem of a young plum or almond tree whose top is cut off once the peach bud starts to grow).

There are several good varieties of peach, but perhaps the best two are Duke of York, which ripens in

July, and Peregrine, which ripens in August. Of the nectarines, Early Rivers and Lord Napier are among the best and will ripen from July to August.

Occasionally the rootstock will send up suckers (shoots from its roots) and these should be pulled out.

Planting

Container-grown peaches may be planted at any time of year; bare root specimens from November to January. Excavate a hole large enough to take all the roots when they are spread out (or the undisturbed rootball) and replace the soil, firming it with your foot. The peach should be planted 15 cm (6 in) away from the wall and the soil level should correspond with the soil mark on the stem. Water well after planting.

Pruning and training

Fan training is the best method to adopt; it is not as daunting as it sounds if you follow these instructions step by step. Your 'maiden' (a one-year-old tree) will have a single stem which will start to grow in early spring. Cut it back to a height of 60 cm (2 ft), and as soon as two good shoots pointing in opposite directions can be seen 23 to 30 cm (9 to 12 in) from the base of the tree, cut back the central stem to them and remove all other shoots.

Fasten a 1.5-m (5-ft) cane to the wires to support each of these shoots. They will be taken upwards at an angle of 45°. All sideshoots which form on these main laterals are pinched out. The following winter shorten each of the main laterals back to about 75 or 100 cm (2½ to 3 ft) and allow four shoots to grow from each of them the following summer, spacing these out on the wire framework. At the end of the year these are also cut back to 75 cm (2½ ft).

During the third summer after planting, new shoots are allowed to grow at 23 cm (9 in) intervals from the top sides of the laterals; all those pointing in other directions being removed. Pinch out the tips of the retained shoots when they reach 45 cm (18 in) and allow the bud left at the tip to grow on and extend the framework.

Peaches fruit on one year old wood and the aim is to produce this in sufficient quantity.

In succeeding years all sideshoots which have carried fruits are cut out as the fruit is picked, and new shoots kept to replace them. Always remove any shoots that grow directly away from the wall, tying and spacing out those to be retained. The thinning of growths is easiest to carry out in spring when the soft green shoots can be pinched off.

Growing conditions

Give plenty of ventilation right through the winter when the trees are dormant, but in February close the vents to keep the trees warmer and start them into growth. Scatter a 10-cm (4-in) potful of general fertilizer on the border around the plant and give the soil a good soak with the hosepipe. A 5-cm (2-in) mulch of well-rotted manure or compost will enrich the soil and keep it moist after watering.

Spray the tree daily with tepid rainwater and maintain temperatures of 10°C (50°F) at night and 16°C (60°F) during the day – ventilating when necessary. Damp down the floor twice a day.

Keep an eye on the soil and soak it with the hosepipe every few weeks when it shows signs of drying out. On no account should the trees go short of water. Shade them from strong sunshine.

Pollination and thinning

When the flowers open dust the pollen from one to another with a soft paintbrush or rabbit's tail to assist pollination. When fruits are the size of marbles thin them out so that they are about 10 cm (4 in) apart. Stop spraying with water at this stage. When they are larger and the stones have formed within them, thin again to leave one every 23 cm (9 in) or so.

Harvesting

Pick the fruits when they are ripe and eat them as soon as possible. Ripe fruits will feel soft on the shoulder (the part nearest the stalk) and should part easily from the tree. Spray the foliage daily with water once all the fruits have been harvested.

Pests, diseases and disorders

Aphids, mildew, peach leaf curl (though this rarely attacks greenhouse-grown trees), red spider mite and scale insects.

Strawberries

Buy some healthy, rooted strawberry runners from a nursery or garden centre in August and pot them up, three to a 20-cm (8-in) pot of JIP 3. Water them in and stand the pots outside for the rest of the year, taking care to see that they are not allowed to dry out.

Bring the plants into the greenhouse in January and maintain a temperature of 10°C (50°F). Gradually increase the temperature to 16°C (60°F) in February. As soon as the plants come into flower, feed them every ten days with diluted liquid fertilizer. Pick all but a dozen fruits on each plant so that you can enjoy delicious strawberries in April and May.

Grow them in a screened-off section of the greenhouse at the heater end so that the whole house does not have to be heated. Discard the plants when they have fruited.

Good varieties

Cambridge Favourite, Tamella, Royal Sovereign.

Pests, diseases and disorders

Aphids and red spider mites.

Strawberries, variety Cambridge Vigour

Vegetables

Not only can you enjoy the more tender varieties of vegetable if you own a greenhouse, but you can also grow some of the hardy types to crop out of season. Just when prices in the shops are at their highest you can be eating home-grown winter lettuce, without even have to provide heat; and in summer exotic aubergines can be yours for the picking.

Cucumbers and tomatoes are not suitable bedfellows if you look at their requirements on paper – the cucumber likes it warm, shady and humid, while the tomato appreciates a little more light and air – but for years they've been grown together with reasonable success, so there is no reason why you shouldn't try them both together.

You'll find capsicums (sweet peppers) very little bother at all, but tomatoes will keep you busy if you want a really good crop.

Salad vegetables can make full use of empty soil borders in winter and spring. Radishes will mature even faster than when sown outdoors, and mustard and cress can be grown through the year on trays of tissue in any spare corner.

With just a little heat some crops can be forced to give their harvest early – potatoes, French beans, chicory and rhubarb are included here, and stretching the title a little, I've included mushrooms.

For details of pests and diseases see pages 112 to 117.

Tomato, variety Ailsa Craig
in growing bags

Aubergine

How to start
Sow a few seeds in a pot of seed compost in January or February and germinate them in a temperature of 16 to 18°C (60 to 65°F). Prick out the seedlings individually into 8-cm (3-in) pots of JIP 1 or a soilless equivalent as soon as they are large enough to handle.

How to grow
Maintain a temperature of 16°C (60°F) and pot on the plants into 12-cm (5-in) pots of JIP 2 or a soilless equivalent when they are ready for a move. Water them well if the compost shows signs of drying out. Pinch out the shoot tip of each plant when it is 12 cm (5 in) high. When the plants have outgrown their 12-cm (5-in) pots, transfer them to 20-cm (8-in) pots of JIP 3 or equivalent.

Spray the open flowers with tepid rainwater to encourage fruit setting and feed the plants every two weeks with diluted liquid tomato fertilizer.

Allow only six to eight fruits to form on each plant. Pinch out any sideshoots to keep the plant shapely. Shade from bright sunshine and ventilate well through the summer.

Harvesting
Pick the fruits when they are large enough and still shiny. Dull-skinned fruits will be tough and unappetising. Discard the plants when all the fruit has been harvested.

Good varieties
Black Prince, Claresse, Long Purple, Moneymaker.

Pests, diseases and disorders
Aphids, red spider mites and whitefly.

Capsicum (Sweet Pepper)

How to start
In March sow the seeds in a pot of seed compost and germinate them in a temperature of 16°C (60°F).

Capsicum, variety Bell Buoy

Prick out the seedlings individually into 8-cm (3-in) pots of JIP 1 or a soilless equivalent as soon as they are large enough to handle.

How to grow
Keep the greenhouse heated to 16 or 18°C (60 or 65°F) and pot on the plants when necessary into 15- or 20-cm (6- or 8-in) pots of JIP 3 or a soilless equivalent. Water thoroughly when the compost looks dry. Pinch out the growing points of the plants when they are 12 cm (5 in) high. When the flowers open spray them with tepid rainwater to encourage fruits to set, and feed once a week with diluted tomato fertilizer. The plants will usually support themselves but provide them with canes if they look like toppling over. Shade from strong sunshine and ventilate well through the summer.

Harvesting
Pick the fruits when they are of a usable size. They will be green at first, turning to bright red, and can be eaten at either stage. If they are allowed to ripen on the plant, growth will slow down and the succeeding fruits may not fully develop. Discard the plants when all the fruits have been picked.

Good varieties
Canape, Early Prolific, New Ace, Worldbeater.

Pests, diseases and disorders
Aphids and red spider mites.

Carrots

How to start
Cultivate the border soil and level it with a rake. Ordinary unmanured soil is quite sufficient. Sow the seeds thinly in 5-mm ($\frac{1}{4}$-in) deep drills spaced 23 cm (9 in) apart. Cover the seeds and water them in.
Sowing time February.

How to grow
Ventilate during bright spells of sunshine and water thoroughly when necessary. Remove weeds as they emerge. Ventilate freely from April onwards. No thinning is

necessary. If the soil is stony or too rich the roots may fork.

Harvesting time
Pull the young carrots when you need them at any time from early May onwards. Take the fattest ones first and leave the thin ones behind to plump up.

Good varieties
Amstel, Early Nantes.

Pests, diseases and disorders
Carrot fly and slugs.

Salad crops

Tomatoes and cucumbers are two of the most popular greenhouse crops but there are a few less obvious salad crops which, although they need little headroom and could manage as well in a frame, can be grown in the greenhouse border when it is standing idle. They can be cleared before the main growing season when the border will be needed for other crops.

Beetroot

How to start
Cultivate the border soil and level it with a rake. Good but not over-rich soil is preferred. Sow the seeds 5 cm (2 in) apart and 2.5 cm (1 in) deep in rows 23 cm (9 in) apart. Water them in.

How to grow
Thin the seedlings to leave them 10 cm (4 in) apart. Water when necessary and ventilate freely from April onwards. Remove any weeds that emerge. If the soil is stony or too rich the roots may fork.

Harvesting time
Pull the roots in June while they are still quite small and tender.

Good varieties
Boltardy, Early Bunch, both sown in February.

Pests, diseases and disorders
Aphids.

Cucumber

How to start

Sow two seeds in an 8-cm (3-in) peat pot of seed compost in March or April and germinate them in a temperature of 18°C (65°F). Remove the weakest seedling after germination, and grow on the remaining one in a temperature of 18°C (65°F).

Cucumber, variety Vercour

How to grow

Attach horizontal training wires to the sides and roof of the greenhouse, spacing them 30 cm (1 ft) apart. The cucumbers can be planted in boxes of JIP 3 in the same way as melons (see page 100), or in growing bags laid on the border or staging, or in mounds of JIP 3 placed directly on the soil border which itself has been enriched with manure or garden compost.

Water the plants before planting, and make sure that the rim of the peat pot is just below the surface of the compost and no deeper. Water the plant in and never allow the compost to dry out.

Tie the stem of each plant to a cane which is led up into the training wires, and pinch out the tips of all sideshoots after two or three leaves have been formed. Stop all subsequent sideshoots after two leaves.

Spray the plants daily with tepid rainwater and damp down the floor.

All male flowers (those which do not have a miniature cucumber behind them) should be removed before they open to prevent pollination. Cucumbers which have developed from fertilized female flowers may be distorted and will taste bitter. All-female varieties do not produce male flowers (or they produce very few) and there is no danger of bitterness. Remove the tendrils whether the plants are mixed gender or all-female.

Shade the plants in summer and ventilate carefully, avoiding draughts. Maintain a temperature of 18 to 20°C (65 to 70°F) during the day, if you can, and 16°C (60°F) at night.

Topdress the surface of the compost with a layer of JIP 3 when fine white roots are seen, and feed once a week from June to September with diluted liquid fertilizer.

Harvesting

Cut the cucumbers as soon as they are large enough to eat – do not leave them on the plant longer than you have to once they are ripe. Clear out the plants and compost when all the fruits have been picked.

Good varieties

Butcher's Disease Resisting, Improved Telegraph. Femdan and Femspot are good all-female varieties.

Pests, diseases and disorders

Aphids, mildew, stem rot, red spider mites and whitefly.

Lettuce

How to start

Fork over the border soil and rake it level. The lettuces will grow best if they follow a well-manured crop such as tomatoes, cucumbers or melons. Take out 5-mm ($\frac{1}{4}$-in) deep drills 30 cm (1 ft) apart and sow the seeds thinly, raking back the soil to cover them. Water the seeds in using a can fitted with a fine rose. Sow frequently in small quantities.

How to grow

Thin the seedlings when they are

Lettuce, variety Kwiek

2·5 cm (1 in) high to leave one lettuce every 23 cm (9 in). Ventilate well and remove weeds. Water when the soil is dry but avoid splashing the leaves.

Good varieties

Kwiek (sow August–September), Kloek (sow August–October) and May Queen (sow October–February).

Harvesting time

Kwiek: November–December; Kloek: November–March; May Queen: March–May.

Pests, diseases and disorders

Aphids, botrytis, mildew and slugs.

Mustard and cress

How to grow

Lay half a dozen paper tissues in the bottom of an old foil pie dish or freezer pack and soak them with water. Pour off the excess and sow the cress seeds evenly but not too thickly on the surface. Place the foil dish underneath the greenhouse staging where it can be kept at a temperature of 13°C (55°F). Cover it with glass and paper. Check it for water daily. Dowse the tissues gently with a watering can fitted with a fine rose if they look dry.

After three days sow the mustard seed in a separate dish and put it under the staging, covering this tray too with glass and paper. As soon as the shoots emerge, remove the coverings and stand the cress on top of the staging. Do the same with the mustard when it germinates. The two will then come to maturity at the same time and can be cut and mixed when the stalks are 3 cm (1½ in) or so long. Keep the tissues moist at all times.

Good varieties
Curled cress, White mustard; both may be sown all the year round.

Pests, diseases and disorders
Damping off.

Radish

How to start
Cultivate the border soil and level it with a rake. Soil manured for a previous crop is best so, like lettuces, radishes can effectively follow tomatoes, cucumbers and melons. Take out drills 1 cm (½ in) deep and 10 cm (4 in) apart, or sow in between lettuce rows. Sow thinly, cover the seeds and water them in.

How to grow
Little care is needed other than an occasional watering and weeding. If sown thinly the crop can be allowed to mature without further thinning. Ventilate well.

Harvesting time
The crop may be ready for harvesting as quickly as three weeks after sowing. Do not leave the radishes in the soil too long after they are ready or they will become woody.

Radish, varieties Saxerre and Yellow Gold

Good varieties
Cherry Belle (round and red), French Breakfast (long, red and white), Long White Icicle (long, white), all sown in early February to March.

Pests, diseases and disorders
Flea bettle.

Tomatoes

How to start
Sow the seeds in mid-March in a pot of seed compost and germinate them in a temperature of 18°C (65°F). As soon as the seedlings are large enough to handle, prick them out individually into 8-cm (3-in) pots of JIP 1 or a soilless equivalent.

How to grow
Tomatoes may be grown in several different ways:

1 They may be planted in 25- or 30-cm (10- or 12-in) pots of JIP 3 and stood on the floor of the greenhouse or on a sheet of polythene stretched over the soil border.

2 They may be planted in growing bags positioned on the floor, the border or the staging.

3 If the ground is in good condition they may be planted in a soil border which has been enriched with well-rotted manure or garden compost and a sprinkling of general fertilizer. (Do not grow them in the same soil for more than two years running.)

4 They may be grown on the ring-culture system.

Ring culture
Place a sheet of polythene over the border soil and cover it with a 15-cm (6-in) layer of washed pea shingle, retained front and back by wooden boards. The tomatoes are planted in 23-cm (9-in) diameter 'rings' containing JIP 3. The rings may be made of aluminium or 'whalehide' (a type of bituminous paper), or from plastic pots which have had their bottoms cut out with a hacksaw. The rings are positioned 45 cm (18 in) apart on the shingle before being filled to within 5 cm

(2 in) of their rims with compost. Plant the young tomatoes when they are 23 cm (9 in) high and water them in – soaking the compost thoroughly. From now on water is applied daily to the bed of shingle and only diluted liquid feed poured on the compost. (The shingle can be used for several seasons if it is flooded clear of impurities each winter.) Peat is sometimes recommended as a substitute for shingle but it can become sour and the tomato leaves will turn yellow as a result.

Tomato, variety Alicante

Growing on
Whatever system you decide to use, water the plants well after planting and provide them with some means of support straight away. Stout 1.5-m (5-ft) canes can be pushed into pots or borders; or strong twine can be fastened to a horizontal wire running down the house 2 m (6 ft) above ground level. The lower end of the twine is held in the compost with a wire peg, and the plant twisted around the twine as it grows. Maintain an average day temperature of 16 to 20°C (60 to 70°F) and a night temperature of 13°C (55°F).

Remove any sideshoots as they emerge and do not allow the compost to dry out at any time. Tie the stem to its cane (or twist it around the twine) as it grows.

As soon as the first truss of flowers opens spray the blooms with water to encourage fruit production. Feed the plants once a week with diluted tomato fertilizer as soon as the fruits start to swell.

Ventilate freely in warm weather and shade lightly in summer to prevent scorching.

Stop the plants by pinching out their growing points as soon as five or six trusses of flowers have opened. One or two leaves can be removed around developing trusses of fruits to allow air circulation. It is quite unnecessary to remove all the lower leaves. Fumigate the greenhouse occasionally to control insect pests.

Harvesting
Pick the fruits as soon as they are ripe. Do not leave them on the plants once they have changed colour.

Stop feeding in September and ease off watering. Pick any unripe fruits in October and store them in a cool place where they will ripen. Pull out the plants and discard the compost. Flood the shingle if plants were grown on the ring culture system.

Good varieties
Ailsa Craig, Alicante, Eurocross BB, Golden Sunrise (yellow) and Moneymaker.

Pests, diseases and disorders
Blotchy ripening, blossom end rot, greenback, eelworm, leaf mould, potato blight, red spider mite, root rot, stem rot, verticillium wilt, virus and whitefly. If this list sounds daunting don't worry – you might not encounter any of them!

Mushrooms

It seems that mushrooms are the orchids of the 'vegetable' world, for they are surrounded with just as much mystery. However it is quite a simple job to produce your own mushrooms at any time of year without going to the expense of buying a tiny plastic bucket full of manure and spawn at an outrageous price.

Preparation for planting
Obtain a few sackfuls of horse manure and tip them into a heap 1 m (3 ft) high in a sheltered place outdoors. Turn the heap every four or five days over a period of three weeks until the manure is darker in colour and more decomposed. Water if it if looks dry.

When it no longer smells of ammonia, tip the manure into 30-cm (1-ft) deep wooden boxes which you should be able to obtain from your local greengrocer. Stand the boxes underneath the greenhouse staging.

Using a soil thermometer (or an ordinary one that you don't mind being dirtied) take the temperature of the manure a few inches below the surface. When it falls to between 20 and 24°C (70 and 75°F) the mushroom spawn can be planted.

How to plant
Blocks of spawn (compacted compost containing the mycelium of the mushroom) can be obtained from garden centres or seed merchants. Break up the block into pieces the size of conkers and plant them 2.5 cm (1 in) deep and 23 cm (9 in) apart in the manure.

Growing on
Maintain a greenhouse temperature of 13 to 16°C (55 to 60°F) and cover the boxes with old sacks or pieces of carpet to create a warm, dark and moist atmosphere.

Mushrooms ready for picking

In two or three weeks' time the surface of the compost will be seen to be covered with thin white threads. This is the 'mycelium' of the mushroom – the fungal equivalent of roots. Cover the surface of the manure with a 2.5-cm (1-in) layer of a mixture of garden soil and peat in equal parts with two or three handfuls of lime added to each bucketful. This mixture is known as the 'casing'.

Keep the casing moist but not wet by spraying it with a plant-mister.

Harvesting
White pinheads should start to appear about three weeks after casing, and the mushrooms will be ready for picking from about four weeks onwards. Pick each mushroom by gently grasping its cap and twisting it away from the cluster of which it is part. It should come away with a few 'roots' and any hole that is left behind should be filled with the casing mixture.

The mushrooms will carry on cropping for two or three months and the boxes can be tipped out and used as garden compost when the supply comes to an end.

If you can't get hold of horse manure or wooden boxes don't despair: you can always resort to the more expensive plastic bucket!

Forced food crops

You don't need much heat to bring some vegetable crops to maturity considerably earlier than normal. These four will offer you a tasty return for the time and trouble you take in growing them.

Chicory

How to grow
Lift chicory roots from the vegetable garden at the end of the growing season, and cut off all but 2.5 cm (1 in) of the foliage. The smaller

roots are also removed, leaving the large, central tap root fairly clean. Store these roots in dry sand in a frost-proof place until you are ready to force them. They can be used over several months.

Pot up three or four roots in a 15-cm (6-in) pot of moist peat and place this under the staging where it can be covered with an inverted pot and some black polythene to exclude light. Maintain a temperature of 10°C (50°F).

Harvesting
Fat, white crispy chicons will appear in about three weeks. Light will turn the chicons green and bitter so take care to black out properly. Discard the roots after forcing.

Good varieties
Witloof, Normato.

Pests, diseases and disorders
None to speak of.

Forced chicory chicons

French beans

How to grow
Sow four seeds in a 15-cm (6-in) pot of JIP 1 at any time from December to February. Water them in and keep the pot at a temperature of 16°C (60°F). Give the young plants good light, support them with small pieces of brushwood and spray them overhead with tepid water when the flowers appear. Feed every ten days with diluted liquid fertilizer from this stage onwards. Water when the compost in the pots is dry.

Dwarf French beans

Harvesting
The beans will be ready for picking ten or twelve weeks after sowing. Pick them regularly.

Good varieties
The Prince, Masterpiece.

Pests, diseases and disorders
Aphids and red spider mite.

Potatoes

How to grow
In January plant three sprouted seed potatoes in a 20-cm (8-in) pot half filled with a mixture of peat and JIP 3 in equal parts. The potatoes should be covered with 5 cm (2 in) of compost. Water them in and place the pots on the greenhouse floor or staging, maintaining a temperature of 10°C (50°F). As the shoots grow, topdress the plants with more

Pot-grown potatoes

compost little by little until the pots are almost full. Given plenty of light and sufficient water the tubers should be ready to harvest in April.

Good varieties
Epicure, Sharpe's Express.

Pests, diseases and disorders
Aphids.

Rhubarb

How to grow
If you have a rhubarb patch in your vegetable garden, dig up one or two fat crowns in November and leave them on the surface of the soil for a few days to become frosted. After this they can be packed quite close together in 20-cm (8-in) deep boxes of moist peat. Water the crowns in and place the boxes underneath the greenhouse staging before covering them with black polythene to exclude light. Support the polythene on canes pushed into either end of the box. Maintain a temperature of 13 to 16°C (55 to 60°F). Lift off the polythene and examine the boxes every week, watering the peat if it looks dry.

Harvesting
Pull the succulent pink sticks of rhubarb when they are about 30 cm (1 ft) long. Discard the crowns when cropping begins to tail off. Boxed up at fortnightly intervals through November and December, rhubarb crowns will provide you with delicious desserts through January and February.

Good varieties
Champagne, Timperley Early.

Pests, diseases and disorders
Aphids and crown rot.

Pests and diseases

Control of pests and diseases

Strong plants which are growing vigorously are far less likely to fall prey to certain diseases, and can stand up much better to attacks from pests. An adequate supply of air, light, moisture and nutrients is essential for growth, and if you propagate from healthy stock at the start your plants will stand every chance of succeeding.

Prevention is always better than cure: keep the greenhouse clean and the plants free of dead leaves and flowers. Discard any plants that are weak or ill. Wash all pots and trays before use and make sure that compost is sterile. Remove all weeds that appear in pots or on the greenhouse floor.

Some plant varieties are resistant to certain diseases and these should be selected – especially if the disease has been encountered previously.

Always use your border soil wisely. Make sure that it is enriched with adequate supplies of well-rotted manure or garden compost, and add fertilizer too. Never grow the same crop in the border for more than two years running, and plant a different crop every year for preference. This 'crop rotation', as it is called, is a sensible practice.

Each winter give the greenhouse a good clear out and a scrub down, ready to start the following spring with a clean bill of health.

When a pest or disease attack is first seen act quickly – a little attention may keep it under control. If you wait a few days before you do anything you may have a disaster on your hands.

Identification

If it moves it's a pest; if it doesn't move it may be a pest, a disease or a disorder.

Pests Most plant pests are insects and can be killed with insecticides.

Mites are controlled with acaricides and slugs and snails with molluscicides – usually mixed with bait and compressed into pellets.

Diseases Fungi, bacteria and viruses are the organisms that cause plant diseases. The first two can usually be controlled by chemical applications or adjustments to cultivation; viruses are not, as a rule, controllable and all plants seen to be infected must be destroyed. Plants propagated from virus-infected stock will be weak and their yield of flowers and fruits very poor.

Disorders Physiological disorders may at first be mistaken for disease, but no fungus, bacteria or virus is in any way responsible for the symptoms shown. Faults in cultivation are to blame, and when growing conditions are adjusted the plants may well be brought back into good health. If you provide a suitable environment from the very beginning disorders can be avoided.

Control measures

There are many ways of controlling pests and diseases – make sure you choose the right method for each particular outbreak.

Hand picking A sprayer is not the only answer to the pest problem. If one plant has half eaten leaves yet all the plants surrounding it are healthy, examine the affected one for caterpillars which can be picked off by hand. Minor infestations of greenfly can be rubbed off with your fingers – a messy but effective means of control on a small scale.

Spraying When large outbreaks of pests or disease have to be dealt with spraying is particularly effective. Soluble powders or liquids are diluted in water and applied to plants with a small hand sprayer or a larger pump-up model fitted with a lance. Apply sprays evenly and make

sure that the undersides of the leaves are coated as thoroughly as the upper surface.

Aerosols The aerosol is an expensive way of buying chemical sprays but no mixing is necessary so it could be thought of as safer. Hold the aerosol at least 30 cm (1 ft) away from the plant before depressing the button, and dispose of the pressurized canister without puncturing as soon as it is empty.

Dusts Although they are less effective than sprays, dusts are useful for treating flowers which could be scorched by liquid applications. Puffer-packs are the most usual means of application, and the aim should be to coat the plant with a thin, even film of dust. When insecticidal dust is to be applied to the soil to control subterranean pests it is usually supplied in a pepper-pot dispenser.

Baits Slugs and snails are usually killed by poisoned baits laid around plants likely to be attacked. Put the pellets under a piece of slate: in the greenhouse there is less likelihood of them being eaten by pets or children, and this protective covering will keep the pellets dry and so make them last longer.

Fumigants One of the easiest ways to control greenhouse pests and fungus diseases is to fumigate. Small firework-like canisters or cones are lit in the sealed greenhouse in the early evening and the poisonous smoke they give off is allowed to hover in the atmosphere all night. The greenhouse can be opened up the following morning as usual.

Check that no pets have found their way into the greenhouse before you fumigate, and make all doors and ventilators as airtight as possible. Do not fumigate in bright sunshine. Nicotine shreds are an alternative to the firework type of fumigant. They look like shredded paper and should be lit and allowed to smoulder (gently stamp out any flames that appear when you are lighting the shreds).

Electric vaporizers These units are fitted to the inside of the greenhouse and can be filled with powder which slowly vaporizes to control pests or diseases. They operate both day and night and the vapour they give off is supposedly harmless to human beings.

Biological control If you are against using chemicals to control pests there are a number of alternative means you can use, including biological control.

Two pests in particular – whitefly and red spider mite – can be kept in check by introducing insect predators to your greenhouse. Whitefly is controlled by a chalcid wasp, *Encarsia formosa*, which lays its eggs in the immature scales of the pest, and red spider mite is attacked by another mite called *Phytoseiulus persimilis*. Neither of these predators attacks plants.

For biological control to be effective you must maintain a certain minimum temperature in your greenhouse at all times (in winter as well as summer) and you must also be prepared to put up with a small number of pests all the time or the predators will run out of food.

The use of insecticidal sprays will be severely limited for these are likely to affect the predators as well as the pests.

Both types of predator, together with full information on how to introduce and maintain them, can be obtained at a modest price from the Royal Horticultural Society's Garden, Wisley, Ripley, Surrey.

Safety precautions
You and your plants should be perfectly safe with chemicals if you observe the following precautions:

1 Read the manufacturer's instructions and follow them carefully.

2 Take the added precaution of wearing a pair of rubber gloves when handling any chemical and wash your hands and face afterwards.

3 Never make a solution more concentrated than the manufacturer recommends – it will damage the plants rather than the pest or disease.

4 Observe the time lapses specified by the manufacturer to be allowed between spraying and harvesting.

5 Insecticides applied to control harmful insects may also kill beneficial ones. Bees are especially susceptible so always spray in the evening when most of them are back in the hive, or on dull days when they are not so active. Where possible choose specific aphicides. These will kill greenfly and blackfly but not bees, lacewings and ladybirds.

6 Avoid mixing more solution than you will need, and dispose of any surplus by flushing it down the lavatory. Empty chemical containers should be capped tightly and put in the dustbin.

7 Store all chemicals in clearly labelled containers out of the reach of children and animals.

Product names
The chemicals mentioned on the following pages are available under various trade names. Your nursery or garden centre will advise on which trade product contains the active ingredient you want, or you can find the information in a booklet entitled 'Directory Of Garden Chemicals', which is available from the British Agrochemicals Association, Alembic House, 93 Albert Embankment, London SE1.

A selection of aids in pest control.

Pests in the greenhouse

Ants
Small, dark brown or orange-brown insects which move very fast.
Attack A wide range of pot- and border-grown plants are affected by their activities.
Damage Soil is disturbed by their nests and greenfly are farmed for honeydew and so encouraged.
Remedy Drench accessible nests with boiling water. Dust with ant powder or lay poisoned jelly baits such as 'Nippon'.

Aphids
This is the collective term for greenfly and blackfly.
Attack A very wide range of plants.
Damage Plants are weakened due to sap being sucked; virus diseases are transmitted; sticky honeydew is secreted which can become infested with sooty mould.
Remedy Small infestations can be rubbed off with the fingers (messy but effective). Spray the plants with pirimicarb, malathion or dimethoate. Fumigate the greenhouse with HCH canisters or nicotine shreds.

Carrot fly
The small white grubs of this fly do the damage.
Attack The roots of carrots.
Damage Roots burrowed into and spoiled; foliage turns red and wilts.
Remedy Dust around the seedlings with bromophos.

Caterpillars
Long grubs of a range of butterflies and moths.
Attack A wide range of plants.
Damage Leaves eaten so that they become covered in holes. Black droppings in evidence.
Remedy Pick off the grubs and destroy them in isolated outbreaks. Spray larger infestations with derris or malathion.

Cutworms
Large creamy white caterpillars found in the soil. Usually curl up when disturbed.
Attack Roots of plants in the border soil.
Damage Plants wilt and generally lose vigour.
Remedy Pick out any grubs found when the border is being cultivated. Fork in bromophos.

Earwigs
Dark brown insects with 'pincer' tails.
Attack Carnations, chrysanthemums and occasionally other plants.
Damage Petals (and occasionally leaves) eaten.
Remedy Dust plants with HCH. Trap the pests in plantpots stuffed with straw and inverted on top of canes pushed among the plants. Empty daily into boiling water.

Eelworms
Minute worm-like insects, usually invisible to the naked eye.
Attack Tomatoes, chrysanthemums, narcissi, potatoes.
Damage Plants lose vigour and will show the following symptoms: Chrysanthemum: leaves turn brown on areas between veins; Narcissi: leaves become distorted; Tomato: roots appear to be knotted; Potatoes: have tiny cysts on the roots.
Remedy Dig up and destroy infected plants (do not use soil border for same crop again). Control weeds which may also act as hosts. Grow different plants in soil borders each year as a means of prevention.

Flea beetle
Tiny black-striped beetles.
Attack Seedlings of members of the cabbage family, turnips and radishes.
Damage Leaves punctured and spotted.

Aphids attacking a tulip

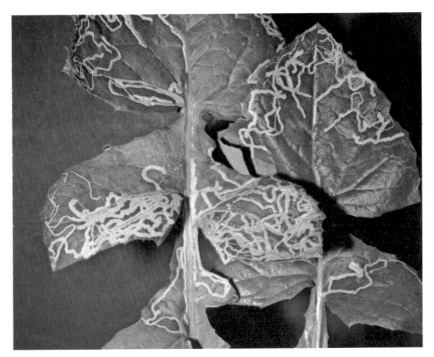

Leaf miner on chrysanthemum leaves

Remedy Keep the seedlings growing vigorously and dust them with derris shortly after they emerge.

Leaf miner
Small cream grubs of certain species of fly.
Attack Chrysanthemums, cinerarias.
Damage White tunnels can be seen under the surface of leaves. The plants are disfigured as a result and if the attack is severe and unchecked the general condition of the plant deteriorates.
Remedy Remove leaves if only a few are affected. Spray larger outbreaks with malathion.

Leatherjackets
Long, grey, legless grubs. Larvae of the 'daddy long-legs'.
Attack Roots of plants growing in the border soil.
Damage Wilting and loss of vigour.
Remedy Fork carbaryl into the border soil.

Mealy bug
Small, oval, white insects surrounded by a woolly deposit.
Attack Grapes, ferns and other ornamental plants.
Damage Reduce plant vigour by sucking sap. Honeydew secreted.
Remedy Fumigate greenhouse with nicotine shreds. Spray infested plants with derris or pyrethrum. Wash off stubborn colonies with cotton-wool soaked in derris.

Red spider mite
Tiny mites the size of a pinhead and coloured cream or reddish brown.
Attack Many greenhouse plants.
Damage Leaves become bleached and mottled. Fine webbing can be seen in severe cases.
Remedy Spraying plants with water will discourage the mites. Fumigate the greenhouse with nicotine. Spray with malathion or dimethoate at fortnightly intervals. Introduce predators.

Scale insects
Small brown dome-shaped scales found on leaves and stems.
Attack Grapes and many other plants.
Damage Sap is sucked and plant vigour reduced. Honeydew secreted.
Remedy Fumigate greenhouse with nicotine. Spray plants with malathion. Wash off stubborn infestations with cotton-wool dipped in diluted malathion.

Slugs and snails
Too well known to need description.
Attack A wide range of plants.
Damage Leaves, stems and roots eaten and slimy trails left behind.
Remedy Lay poisoned pellets out of the reach of pets (or simply keep pets out of the greenhouse). Yoghurt cartons half filled with beer and sunk into the ground make good traps.

Thrips
Small dark brown insects.
Attack Carnations, chrysanthemums and other plants.
Damage Suck the sap from leaves and flowers causing them to become distorted and streaked.
Remedy Keep the greenhouse well ventilated and spray plants with water to discourage the pest. fumigate the greenhouse with nicotine. Spray plants with malathion.

Whitefly
Small white flies with folded wings – usually colonize on undersides of leaves. Immature stages are in the form of small white scales.
Attack Tomatoes, cucumbers and a wide range of ornamental plants.
Damage Sap is sucked and the plants are weakened.
Remedy Spray plants with malathion or resmethrin at fortnightly intervals to kill emerging adults. Introduce predators.

Diseases and disorders

Botrytis (blackleg or grey mould)
Stems rot and turn black at soil level and plants die as a result. Stems and leaves may rot off and develop a grey, fluffy outgrowth.
Attacks Many plants, but especially pelargoniums, tomatoes, cucumbers and melons.
Remedy Ventilate well whenever possible to avoid a stagnant, humid atmosphere. This disease is prevalent in winter. Fumigate with tecnazene. Spray with captan. Destroy infected plants. Remove all faded flowers and leaves and keep the greenhouse clean.

Blossom end rot
Tomatoes develop sunken black blotches at the end furthest from the stalk.
Attacks Only tomatoes.
Remedy A disorder caused by dryness at the roots. Keep the soil just moist at all times.

Blotchy ripening
Uneven coloured fruits blotched with red, green and yellow.
Attacks Only tomatoes.
Remedy A disorder caused by lack of potash in the soil. Dress soil borders with sulphate of potash at 30 g per sq m (1 oz per sq yd). Water container-grown plants with tomato fertilizer which will contain potash.

Chlorosis
Plants become stunted and foliage turns yellow.
Attacks A wide range of plants.
Remedy A disorder caused by a shortage of magnesium or iron. Often a problem in chalky soils. Water affected plants with diluted iron sequestrene. Check that soil is well supplied with nutrients from the start.

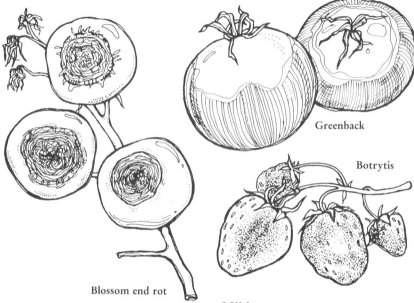

Blossom end rot

Greenback

Botrytis

Damping off
Seedlings fall over due to bases of stems rotting.
Attacks A wide range of seedlings.
Remedy Ventilate well whenever possible. This fungus disease thrives in a humid, stagnant atmosphere. Sow seeds thinly to prevent overcrowding and water with Cheshunt compound in early stages.

Galls
Distorted outgrowths at the base of the stem.
Attack Pelargoniums, chrysanthemums, dahlias.
Remedy Propagate from healthy plants in the first place. Discard infected plants.

Greenback
Upper surface of the fruit stays green and does not ripen.
Attacks Tomatoes.
Remedy Choose resistant varieties. Ensure adequate potash in soil (see blotchy ripening). Shade plants from very strong sunshine.

Mildew
Whitish powdery deposit on leaves and stems. Eventually turns brown and tissue rots.
Attacks Wide range of plants including grapes, chrysanthemums, lettuces and cinerarias.
Remedy Ventilate well whenever possible to keep air circulating. Spray with benomyl. Fumigate with dinocap.

Peach leaf curl
Leaves become curled and puckered, turning red as they do so. They fall prematurely and stems become weak and spindly.
Attacks Peaches and nectarines (but only rarely when they are grown in a greenhouse).
Remedy Spray with Bordeaux mixture in February as the buds begin to swell. Pick infected leaves.

Potato blight
Fruits develop dark brown areas and eventually rot.
Attacks Tomatoes (potatoes outdoors are also affected – the foliage and tubers turning brown).
Remedy Spray tomatoes with zineb

in early July if the disease has previously been a problem. Dig up and destroy all infected plants.

Root rot
Shoot tips of infected plants wilt and eventually the plant collapses entirely.
Attacks Tomatoes.
Remedy Water carefully at all times so that plants are kept just moist. Keep the temperature sufficiently high. Topdress infected plants with peaty compost, shade from strong sunshine and spray with tepid water to encourage new root growth.

Rust
Orange or brown spots develop on the leaves.
Attacks Pelargoniums, antirrhinums, chrysanthemums, carnations.
Remedy Pick off and destroy infected leaves. Spray with zineb or thiram at

fortnightly intervals. Grow resistant varieties of antirrhinum.

Scalding
Fruits turn brown on one side.
Attacks Grapes.
Remedy Caused by bright sun shining on the fruits so check that shading is in position on sunny days.

Shanking
Fruit stalks shrivel and the berries subsequently wither.
Attacks Grapes.
Remedy Thin the bunches properly and make sure that the border soil is well drained.

Sooty mould
Black, felt-like outgrowth on the surface of leaves and stems. Cuts out light and so weakens the plant.
Attacks A wide range of plants.
Remedy Control aphids, mealy bugs

and scale insects which secrete honeydew on which the mould grows. Remove the mould with cotton-wool or a sponge dipped in water.

Stem rot
Stem rots just above ground level and the plant collapses.
Attacks Tomatoes, cucumbers and melons.
Remedy Grow the plants in a sufficiently high temperature. Water carefully without splashing. Avoid planting cucumbers and melons too deeply.

Tomato leaf mould
Yellow spots appear on the leaves and enlarge to form a rusty-coloured mould.
Attacks Tomatoes.
Remedy Grow resistant varieties. Ventilate well to prevent a stagnant atmosphere. Spray outbreaks with thiram.

Virus diseases
Leaves may be mottled with yellow, distorted, crinkled and malformed. The plant becomes ugly and is weakened by the disease.
Attacks A wide range of plants.
Remedy Destroy all infected plants. Never propagate from plants which do not appear to be healthy.

Wilt
Plants wilt from the bottom upwards (unlike root rot where the reverse happens). They may recover temporarily only to wilt again. This disease is also known as verticillium or 'sleepy disease'.
Attacks Tomatoes.
Remedy Grow the plants in good soil, keep them warm and shaded from bright sunshine. Spray them daily with tepid water. Destroy all infected plants and drench the soil with Cheshunt compound. Do not grow tomatoes on ground known to have been previously infected.

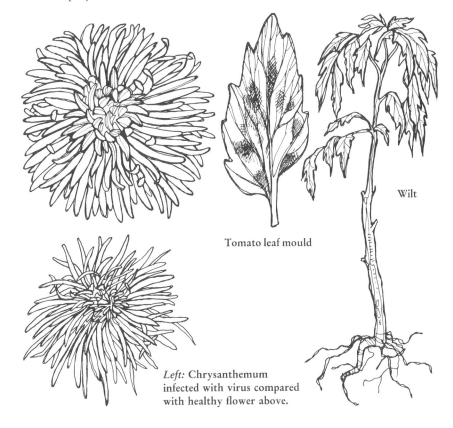
Tomato leaf mould

Left: Chrysanthemum infected with virus compared with healthy flower above.

Wilt

Greenhouse diary

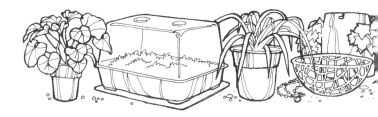

January

Close down the greenhouse at night to protect tender plants, and ventilate carefully in sunny spells during the day. Water cautiously. Wash down the greenhouse inside and out. Wash all pots and trays not in use.

Flowers
Sow Cape primrose, gloxinia, pelargonium.
Plant Hippeastrum.
Take cuttings of Carnations, chrysanthemums.

Buy rooted carnation cuttings. Remove all faded leaves and flowers from pot plants to prevent fungal attacks.

Fruit
Plant Grape vines, peaches and nectarines (bare root).

Bring August-potted strawberries into the greenhouse. Start grapes into growth if you can afford the heat.

Vegetables
Sow French beans, lettuce, mustard and cress.
Plant Mushroom spawn.

Pot up and force chicory and potatoes.

Plants in bloom
African violet, busy lizzie, camellia, carnation, cineraria, cyclamen, freesia, hyacinths, *Jasminum primulinum*, narcissi, pelargonium, ornamental pepper (berries), primulas.

Fruit and vegetables to harvest
Chicory, lettuce, mushrooms, mustard and cress, rhubarb.

February

Keep the greenhouse closed at night but ventilate when possible during the day. Continue to water with care and avoid splashing leaves and flowers.

Flowers
Sow African violet, Cape primrose, gloxinia, pelargonium, ornamental pepper.
Plant Hippeastrum.
Take cuttings of Carnation, chrysanthemum.

Buy rooted carnation cuttings. Continue to remove all faded leaves and flowers.

Fruit
Plant Grape vines (bare root).

Train vine shoots as they grow in heated greenhouses; pollinate the flowers when they open. Start peaches and nectarines into growth.

Vegetables
Sow Aubergines, French beans, beetroot, carrots, lettuce, mustard and cress, radish.
Plant Mushroom spawn.

Pot up and force chicory.

Plants in bloom
African violet, busy lizzie, camellia, carnation, cineraria, cyclamen, freesia, hyacinths, *Jasminum primulinum*, mimosa, narcissi, pelargonium, ornamental pepper (berries), primulas, tulips.

Fruit and vegetables to harvest
Chicory, lettuce, mushrooms, mustard and cress, rhubarb.

March

Apply a little more heat where bedding and greenhouse plants are being raised from seed. Ventilate carefully during the day. Shade newly germinated seedlings from bright sunshine. Damp down from the middle of the month onwards. Plants will need more water. Fumigate if necessary.

Flowers
Sow Abutilon, African violet, asparagus ferns, busy lizzie, Cape primrose, coleus, cup and saucer vine, gloxinia, mimosa, morning glory, pelargonium, ornamental pepper, poor man's orchid, *Primula obconica*, silk oak, bedding plants.
Plant Hippeastrum.

Buy rooted chrysanthemum and carnation cuttings.

Fruit
Sow Melons.
Plant Grape vines (bare root).

Train vine shoots as they grow. Train the shoots on peaches and nectarines and pollinate the flowers. Feed strawberries.

Vegetables
Sow Aubergine, capsicum, cucumber, mustard and cress, radish, tomato.
Plant Mushroom spawn.

Pot up and force chicory.

Plants in bloom
African violet, busy lizzie, camellia, carnation, cineraria, freesia, hippeastrum, hyacinths, *Jasminum polyanthum*, mimosa, narcissi, pelargonium, poor man's orchid, primulas, tulips.

Fruit and vegetables to harvest
Chicory, lettuce, mushrooms, mustard and cress, radish.

April

Damp down morning and evening and shade when necessary during the day. Ventilate carefully. Water plants freely when they are dry. Spray or fumigate if pests and diseases are a problem. Remove any insulating material from the inside of the greenhouse.

Flowers
Sow Abutilon, asparagus ferns, busy lizzie, cineraria, coleus, cup and saucer vine, mimosa, morning glory, ornamental pepper, poor man's orchid, *Primula obconica,* silk oak. *Take cuttings of* Fuchsia, jasmine, pelargonium, pilea, stephanotis.

Divide clump-forming pot plants. Buy rooted chrysanthemum cuttings. Pot on plants that have outgrown their containers. Prick out seedlings.

Fruit
Sow Melons.

Start grapes into growth in unheated greenhouses. Thin the fruits on peaches and nectarines. Plant melons sown in March.

Vegetables
Sow Mustard and cress.

Plant cucumbers sown in March, tomatoes and mushroom spawn.

Plants in bloom
African violet, annuals in pots, busy lizzie, carnation, cineraria, freesia, hippeastrum, *Jasminum polyanthum,* mimosa, narcissi, poor man's orchid, pelargonium, slipper flower, stephanotis, tulips.

Fruit and vegetables to harvest
Chicory, lettuce, mushrooms, mustard and cress, potatoes, strawberries.

May

Water growing plants freely and start to feed them. Shading can be left in position if required. Damp down morning and evening. Ventilate freely and turn off heating during the day if the weather is warm. Spray or fumigate when necessary.

Flowers
Sow Busy lizzie, cineraria, *Primula malacoides,* silk oak, slipper flower. *Take cuttings of* Coleus, fuchsia, ivy, jasmine, pelargonium, pilea, stephanotis.

Divide clump-forming pot plants. Pot up rooted cuttings and continue to pot on plants as they grow. Prick out seedlings. Transfer bedding plants to frame.

Fruit
Continue to train grape vines and pollinate the flowers of those being grown in unheated greenhouses. Thin the fruits of peaches and nectarines. Plant melons sown in April and pollinate those sown in March.

Vegetables
Sow Mustard and cress.
Plant cucumbers sown in April, and mushroom spawn. Train tomatoes.

Plants in bloom
African violet, annuals in pots, bottle brush tree, busy lizzie, carnation, cineraria, hippeastrum, *Jasminum polyanthum,* pelargonium, poor man's orchid, slipper flower, stephanotis.

Fruit and vegetables to harvest
French beans, carrots, lettuce, mushrooms, mustard and cress, potatoes, strawberries.

June

Heating can be turned off this month except with plants that need high temperatures. Continue to damp down, shade, feed and water regularly. Ventilate freely during the day and just a little at night. Spray or fumigate when necessary.

Flowers
Sow Busy lizzie, cineraria, *Primula malacoides,* silk oak, slipper flower. *Take cuttings of* African violet, *Begonia rex,* busy lizzie, Cape primrose, coleus, fuchsia, gloxinia, ivy, pelargonium, pilea.

Divide clump-forming pot plants. Stand carnations, chrysanthemums and summer-hardy pot plants outdoors. Pot up rooted cuttings and continue to pot on plants as they grow.

Fruit
Continue to train grape vines and thin the fruits of those in unheated greenhouses. Train peaches, nectarines and melons. Pollinate April-sown melons and feed every ten days.

Vegetables
Sow Mustard and cress.

Train cucumbers and tomatoes and feed weekly. Plant mushroom spawn.

Plants in bloom
African violet, annuals in pots, bottle brush tree, bougainvillea, busy lizzie, Cape primrose, carnation, fuchsia, gloxinia, hippeastrum, *Jasminum polyanthum,* pelargonium, stephanotis.

Fruit and vegetables to harvest
French beans, beetroot, carrots, grapes (from heated greenhouse), mushrooms, mustard and cress.

July

Water freely, twice a day if necessary. Continue to shade, feed and damp down regularly. The greenhouse door may be fastened open during the day and ventilators should be left open a little at night. Spray or fumigate if pests and diseases are a problem.

Flowers
Sow Silk oak, slipper flower.
Take cuttings of Abutilon, African violet, *Begonia rex*, bottle brush tree, bougainvillea, busy lizzie, camellia, Cape primrose, coleus, cup and saucer vine, fuchsia, gloxinia, ivy, mimosa, passion flower, pelargonium, pila, wax plant.

Divide clump-forming pot plants. Pot up rooted cuttings and pot on plants as they grow.

Fruit
Continue to train grape vines, peaches, nectarines and melons. Support melons in nets and feed every ten days; topdress when necessary.

Vegetables
Sow Mustard and cress.

Train cucumbers and tomatoes and feed weekly; topdress when necessary. Plant mushroom spawn.

Plants in bloom
African violet, bottle brush tree, bougainvillea, busy lizzie, Cape primrose, carnation, cup and saucer vine, fuchsia, gloxinia, morning glory, passion flower, pelargonium, poor man's orchid, stephanotis, wax plant.

Fruit and vegetables to harvest
Capsicum, cucumber, grapes (from heated greenhouses), mushrooms, mustard and cress, nectarines, peaches, tomatoes.

August

Continue to check plants for water twice a day. Shade, feed and damp down regularly. Ventilate well day and night. Spray or fumigate if pests and diseases are a problem.

Flowers
Sow Annuals for a spring display, cyclamen, poor man's orchid.
Plant Freesias, narcissi (late in month).
Take cuttings of Abutilon, African violet, *Begonia rex*, bottle brush tree, bougainvillea, busy lizzie, camellia, Cape primrose, cup and saucer vine, fuchsia, mimosa, passion flower, pelargonium, wax plant.

Pot up rooted cuttings and pot on plants as they grow.

Fruit
Pot up strawberries for spring forcing and stand them outdoors. Continue to train vines, peaches, nectarines and melons. Ease off watering melons as they ripen.

Vegetables
Sow Lettuce, mustard and cress.
Plant mushroom spawn.

Train cucumbers and tomatoes and feed weekly.

Plants in bloom
African violet, bougainvillea, busy lizzie, Cape primrose, carnation, cup and saucer vine, fuchsia, gloxinia, morning glory, passion flower, pelargonium, poor man's orchid, stephanotis, wax plant.

Fruit and vegetables to harvest
Aubergine, capsicum, cucumber, grapes, melons, mushrooms, mustard and cress, nectarines, peaches, tomatoes.

September

Ventilate more cautiously at night but freely on warm days. Remove permanent shading towards the middle of the month. Continue to water and damp down freely. Stop feeding later in the month. A little heat may be needed at night. Fumigate to control pests and diseases.

Flowers
Sow Annuals for a spring display.
Plant Freesias, hyacinths, narcissi, tulips.
Take cuttings of Pelargonium.

Bring carnations, chrysanthemums and other frost-tender plants back into the greenhouse if they have been standing outdoors through the summer. Plunge winter- and spring-flowering bulbs. Pot up rooted cuttings.

Fruit
Continue to train grape vines, peaches and nectarines. Ease off watering melons as they ripen.

Vegetables
Sow Lettuce, mustard and cress.
Plant mushroom spawn.

Train cucumbers and tomatoes and feed weekly.

Plants in bloom
African violet, bougainvillea, busy lizzie, Cape primrose, carnation, cup and saucer vine, fuchsia, morning glory, pelargonium, ornamental pepper (berries), passion flower.

Fruit and vegetables to harvest
Aubergine, capsicum, cucumber, grapes, melons, mushrooms, mustard and cress, tomatoes.

October

Water plants more sparingly this month and stop damping down. Heat greenhouses where tender plants are being grown day and night. Ventilate cautiously during the day.

Flowers
Plant Hippeastrum (prepared), hyacinths, narcissi, tulips.

Plunge winter- and spring-flowering bulbs. Pot up rooted cuttings. Pot up annuals for a spring display.

Fruit
Prepare ground for planting grape vines, peaches and nectarines. Allow the soil around existing vines to become drier.

Vegetables
Sow Lettuce, mustard and cress.
Plant Mushroom spawn.

Plants in Bloom
African violet, busy lizzie, carnation, chrysanthemum, pelargonium, ornamental pepper (berries).

Fruit and vegetables to harvest
Grapes, mushrooms, mustard and cress, tomatoes.

November

Try to maintain a drier atmosphere. Ventilate during the day whenever possible. Heating will be needed day and night by frost-tender plants but fruit trees and vines should not be given any heat at all. Water sparingly and avoid splashing the leaves of plants. Apply insulating material to the inside of the greenhouse.

Flowers
Plant Hippeastrum (prepared), tulips.

Plunge spring-flowering bulbs. Remove faded leaves and flowers from all plants.

Fruit
Plant Grape vines, peaches and nectarines (bare root).
Prune Peaches and nectarines.

Allow grape vines to rest.

Vegetables
Sow Lettuce, mustard and cress.
Plant Mushroom spawn.

Pot up and force chicory. Box up and force rhubarb.

Plants in bloom
African violet, busy lizzie, carnation, chrysanthemum, cineraria, pelargonium, ornamental pepper (berries), primulas.

Fruit and vegetables to harvest
Chicory, lettuce, mushrooms, mustard and cress.

December

Ventilate cautiously during the day whenever the weather is reasonable. Keep floors and staging dry and water plants sparingly. Dust overwintering pot plants with a fungicide such as captan to prevent fungal attack.

Flowers
Take cuttings of Carnations.

Remove faded leaves and flowers from all plants.

Fruit
Plant Grape vines, peaches and nectarines (bare root).
Prune Grape vines.

Ventilate greenhouses where grape vines, peaches and nectarines are being grown.

Vegetables
Sow French beans, lettuce, mustard and cress.
Plant Mushroom spawn.

Pot up and force chicory. Box up and force rhubarb.

Plants in bloom
African violet, busy lizzie, camellia, carnation, chrysanthemum, cineraria, cyclamen, freesia, hippeastrum (prepared), hyacinths, pelargonium, narcissi, ornamental pepper (berries), primulas.

Fruit and vegetables to harvest
Chicory, lettuce, mushrooms, mustard and cress.

List of suppliers

Alpines
Broadwell Nursery, Broadwell, Moreton-in-Marsh, Gloucestershire

Jack Drake, Inshriach Alpine Plant Nursery, Aviemore, Inverness-shire

C. G. Hollett, Greenbank Nursery, Sedbergh, Cumbria

W. E. Th. Ingwersen, Birch Farm Nursery, Gravetye, East Grinstead, West Sussex

Dahlias
Aylett Nurseries Ltd., North Orbital Road, London Colney, St Albans, Hertfordshire

Three Counties Nurseries, Marshwood, Bridport, Dorset

Oscroft's, Spotboro' Road, Doncaster, Yorkshire

Carnations
Allwood Bros, Clayton Nursery, Hassocks, West Sussex

Steven Bailey Ltd, Eden Nurseries, Sway, Hampshire

Pelargoniums
Clipton Geranium Nurseries, Cherry Orchard Road, Whyke, Chichester, Sussex

D. Gamble & Sons, Highfield Nurseries, Longford, Derbyshire

Streptocarpus
Efenechtyd Nurseries, Efenechtyd, Ruthin, Clwyd

Bulbs
Walter Blom & Sons Ltd, Coombelands Nurseries, Leavesden, Watford, Hertfordshire

Michael Jefferson-Brown, Maylite, Martley, Worcester (Daffodils)

Broadleigh Gardens, Barr House, Bishop's Hull, Taunton, Somerset

Van Tubergen, Willowbank Wharf, Ranelagh Gardens, London SW6 3JY

Seeds
Chiltern Seeds, Sunnymede Avenue, Chesham, Buckinghamshire (unusual types)

Thomas Butcher Ltd, 60 Wickham Road, Shirley, Croydon, Surrey

Samuel Dobie & Son Ltd, Upper Dee Mills, Llangollen, Clwyd

Hurst, Gunson, Cooper Taber Ltd, Witham, Essex

Sutton & Sons Ltd, Hele Road, Torquay, Devon

W. J. Unwin Ltd, Histon, Cambridge

M. Holtzhausen, 14 High Cross Street, St Austell, Cornwall (unusual types)

African Violets
Tony Clements, African Violet Nurseries, Terrington St Clement, Kings Lynn, Norfolk

Cacti and other Succulents
Holly Gate Nurseries Ltd, Ashington, Sussex

Abby Brook Cactus Nursery, Old Hackney Lane, Matlock, Derbyshire

Strawberries
Ken Muir, Honeypot Farm, Weeley Heath, Clacton-on-Sea, Essex

Potatoes
Donald MacLeon, Dornock Farm, Crieff, Perthshire

Fuchsias
Markham Grange Nursery, Long Lands Lane, Brodsworth, Doncaster, Yorkshire

Wills Fuchsias Ltd, The Fuchsia Nursery, Chapel Lane, West Wittering, Chichester, Sussex

Chrysanthemums
Riley's Chrysanthemums, Alfreton Nurseries, Woolly Moor, Derby

Harold Walker, Oatfield Nurseries, Huntingdon, Chester

H. Woolman (Dorridge) Ltd, Grange Road, Dorridge, Solihull, West Midlands

Camellias
James Trehane & Sons Ltd, Camellia Nursery, Stapehill Road, Hampreston, Wimborne, Dorset

Shrubs and Climbers
Notcutts Nurseries, Woodbridge, Suffolk

Hillier & Sons, Winchester, Hampshire

Fruit trees and Grapes
Scotts Nurseries (Merriott) Ltd, Merriott, Somerset

Thomas Rivers & Son Ltd, The Nurseries, Sawbridgemouth, Hertfordshire

General Greenhouse Plants
B. Wall, 4 Selborne Close, New Haw, Addlestone, Weybridge, Surrey

Fibrox Nurseries Ltd, Harvey Road, Evesham, Worcestershire (including ferns)

Orchids
MacBeans Orchids Ltd, Cooksbridge, Lewes, Sussex

Mansell & Hatcher Ltd, Cragg Wood Nurseries, Rawdon, Leeds, West Yorkshire

Burnham Nurseries Ltd, Orchid Avenue, Kingsteignton, Newton Abbot, Devon

Index